THIS BOOK IS A GIFT FOR:

_____

FROM:

_____

This book is dedicated to our traveling daughters
Heather and Jennifer
for teaching us the pure enjoyment of adventuring as a family!

LESSONS

FROM FAMILY VACATIONS

Trips That Transform

RICK TOCQUIGNY
WITH CARLA TOCQUIGNY

TAYLOR TRADE PUBLISHING
Lanham • Boulder • New York • London

Published by Taylor Trade Publishing
An imprint of The Rowman & Littlefield Publishing Group, Inc.
4501 Forbes Boulevard, Suite 200, Lanham, Maryland 20706
www.rowman.com

Unit A, Whitacre Mews, 26-34 Stannery Street, London SE11 4AB, United Kingdom

Distributed by NATIONAL BOOK NETWORK

British Library Cataloguing in Publication Information Available

Library of Congress Cataloging-in-Publication Data Available
ISBN 978-1-63076-081-6 (cloth : alk. paper) ISBN 978-1-63076-082-3 (electronic)

The paper used in this publication meets the minimum requirements of American National Standard for Information Sciences—Permanence of Paper for Printed Library Materials, ANSI/NISO Z39.48-1992.

Printed in the United States of America

CONTENTS

Acknowledgments   8

Introduction   10

Our Manifesto   12

PACK YOUR BAGS

1   And So We Begin Our Own Style of Travel   14

2   How You Travel Really Matters   18

3   The Road We Take Makes Us   22

4   Pack Your Sense of Humor   26

CHANGED PERSPECTIVE

5   Preserving a Fabled Village   34

6   Oh, the View Is Tremendous   38

7   Protect What You Love   42

8   Staying Alive   46

9   Travel Inspires Design   50

10 We Are the Poor Ones   54

11   Journal Your Adventure   58

12 The Ace Negotiator   64

13 Elephants Stood Vigil   68

14 *Disponible*   72

15 Let Go Completely to Be Fully Alive   76

SENSORY TRAVEL

16	It's So Common Sensory	80
17	Carry a Sense of Home with You	84
18	Music to Our Ears	88
19	Meeting New People	92
20	Awaken Your Nose	96
21	Panama Hats . . . Made with Pride	100
22	The Childlike Feeling of Reverence	104
23	Stumbling Upon Happiness	108

TRAVEL COMPANIONS

24	Spent	112
25	Staying Youthful	118
26	This Is a Test, Only a Test	122
27	I Wish I Would Have Known You Sooner	126
28	The Endurance Test	130
29	Stopping for Directions	134

HOW YOU TRAVEL MATTERS

30	A Giving Community	140
31	Curious Separate Realities	144
32	You Get What You Get	148
33	The Little Brown Ice Chest	152

34 Objects of Affection   158
35 Change Your Place and Change Your Happiness   162
36 Working Vacations   166
37 It's Dollars to Doughnuts at Our State Fair   170
38 Travel for Good Health   174
39 The World Needs Your Random Acts of Kindness   178
40 History Comes to Life   182
41 The Pursuit of Tasteful Knowledge   186
42 Body Clocks   190
43 Treating Others Like Family   194

THE NEXT JOURNEY
44 It's Time for a Family Vacation   198
45 The ABCs for Traveling throughout Your Life —
    from the *Transformed Traveler* Show   202
46 Impermanence   204
47 Choose Wisely—This Could Be Your Last
    Family Vacation   208
48 Great Trip, Dad, Where to Next?   214
49 Writing Their Own Travel Stories   218

Epilogue   222

Acknowledgments

And without you . . .

The team at Taylor Trade Publishing I count as friends. Thanks to *Rick Rinehart* for believing in this book and the entire series.

Copyeditor *April LeHoullier* was instrumental in catching our phrasing and correcting grammar. Thanks for delivering a superlative finished product.

Julia Hulling creatively designed this book. We are so appreciative of her artistic gifts and ability to match visuals with our stories.

The marketing of every Life Lessons book to the right audience is extraordinarily important to our success. To *Kalen Landow* and *Jessica Defranco*, your professional approach made a significant difference.

I am grateful to *Melissa McComas*, my literary agent, for her support and strategic leadership over the Life Lessons enterprise.

To my daughters, *Heather* and *Jennifer*, who have served as idea editors for this book and have been "transformational" examples of excellence.

To our parents, sisters *Nancy* and *Suzanne*, and brothers *George* and *Dennis* for your traveling companionship throughout our family vacations across America.

Thanks to our traveling friends, *Sue* and *Steve Lundgren*, and *Rosalie* and *Ken Asarch*, who continue to inspire us with their own stories.

To the contributing storytellers of Life Lessons including Chrys and John Howard, Al Roker, David Morris, John Glenn, and many others. You have enriched our lives with your tales.

Our special thanks to fine artists Deb Strain and Annie LaPoint for their refreshing art used inside our book depicting a happy camper attitude.

To AAA and their fifty-three million members for supporting our *Transformed Traveler* show and Life Lessons series.

To Samsonite for their support of the *Transformed Traveler* show.

To the many guests on our *Transformed Traveler* show that continue to inspire us including Seth Kugel, Bruce Poon Tip, Simon Veness, Dr. Toni Neuberger, Laureen Ong, Greg Sullivan, Ellen Asmodeo, Stephen Oddo, and so many other talented contributors around the world.

And thanks to God for giving us ears to hear, eyes to see, sense and sensibility, and an ability to express stories that you as an audience can enjoy.

INTRODUCTION

We are delighted to share with you a special gift—*Life Lessons from Family Vacations*. These stories were written to prompt your own unique appreciation for travel time with family.

In writing this book it became clear that family vacations rank as top memory-making moments for families. These milestone events for families are transformations of the human heart and spirit.

The central teacher of this book is travel. Through *Life Lessons from Family Vacations* you will "enjoy the road of experiences" that have changed our lives irrevocably. The tales are as broad and varied as earth's horizon, carrying a common theme that families are utterly changed by vacation experiences.

Many stories reflect the extraordinary effect of togetherness. **Travel draws us closer to understand ourselves and each other, connecting us to nature and often bringing many closer to their Creator.**

In writing this book, we learned that the origin of the word "holiday" means "holy day." Believe it or not, 25 percent of the American workforce does not get paid holidays. In contrast, people living and employed in the European Union are given a minimum of twenty days off, fully paid. No wonder they consider their one month per year as holy! In further contrast, we discovered that Americans are not taking their full vacations earned. Why not take the other four days of vacation owed to you?

That's a hard lesson—we are given time with our family and we don't take advantage of this gift.

Because of family travel,
a deeper part of ourselves is released.
Time shared together is unplugged,
unhurried, more compassionate, and
even more blissful. Taken together,
family vacations are good for your
heart, bodies, and souls.

We end each vacation tale with "And at the end of the journey," expressing a timeless and universal lesson that can be applied to your own families.

Most importantly, we hope that the stories help you unpack your own family vacation memories and relive them with friends and loved ones.

Please feel free to read this book and share the lessons in whatever manner works best for you. Skip around, go from front to back, binge read, or enjoy one lesson at a time. This is your book, and we hope it motivates you to write your own travel tales. *May you bask in the memories of your favorite family vacations.*

Our Manifesto

Families and travel are two of our favorite words. Family evokes a unit of loved ones and travel puts that unit into motion.

Our family manifesto has been written around travel. We use this "constitution" because we know that life lessons will always come from travel. Sure, there are other sources for life lessons such as school, work, marriage, and friendships. We just happen to focus on travel.

This is our life, and we choose to travel. Travel is what we love and we do it often. If you don't have enough time to travel, examine how you are spending your life and rearrange it for travel. Enjoy the people you meet when you are on an adventure. Their stories and lessons are like no others. Everyone has a different perspective on life depending on where they have lived, what they have read, who they have known, and how much they have traveled. Every journey represents an opportunity for you to tap into a new story and make a new friend. It's the people you meet and the life you create with them that really matters.

Travel shows us that the world is actually quite small and that we can be united in our differences. The need for water, food, and love are three simple examples.

Traveling often means awakening all of your five senses and forever being changed by the aroma of a beautiful field of flowers, the taste of a home-cooked meal in a foreign land, listening to the sounds of singing children in a church, seeing the beauty of a sunset across the mountains or sea, and engaging with locals as they touch our hearts.

Getting lost is a good thing. We believe that traveling helps you find your true self, shaping your character along the way.

Because life is short, we choose to travel and share our life lessons from the adventure with the world. Perhaps our passion can become a part of yours.

SECTION ONE
PACK YOUR BAGS

* Life Lesson #1 *

AND SO WE BEGIN OUR OWN STYLE OF TRAVEL

With the newly established interstate highway system in the late 1950s, we became part of the *"see the U.S.A. in your Chevrolet"* generation.

Traveling with your family meant enduring a crowded car with windows rolled down, feet atop one another with sweet memories of stopping at Stuckey's and rest stops. Married in 1979, we began our marriage vowing to create two distinct travel holidays each year. We started with trips around the United States and went coast to coast for ten years before venturing off to Europe in 1989.

In an effort to quell our overseas travel anxiety, we made one long-distance phone call to Germany to book a hotel for our first night.

Upon arrival in this enchanting town of Ulm, we found our hotel décor uninspiring and inconveniently located in the noisiest section of town, next door to the train station.

Making a quick escape the following morning, we hopped on the Autobahn and drove through the scenic German countryside, abundantly awash in wildflowers. As this beautiful day came to a close and long shadows stretched across the roads, we stopped in a small village.

Watching for signs, we parked the car and walked to a small farmhouse. After a quick knock on the door, the proprietor opened his entrance and Carla asked, *"Haben ze doppelzimmer?"* *"Yah, yah,"* said the gentleman.

Clambering up the narrow staircase to the third floor, our gracious host opened the door to our moonlit room. With a ceiling covered in light blue wallpaper accented by tiny flowers, we proceeded to unpack and open the windows. The cows were coming in from a day out to pasture, jangling their bells around their necks.

Hopping on the bed, we experienced German feather comforters for the first time in our lives. "Are you supposed to sleep on top or under this?" we mused. We were limited to ribbed cord bedspreads!

Combine that with our first ever European breakfast, and we were magically transformed into another world.

"We cannot grow, we cannot achieve authentic discovery and our eyes cannot be cleansed to the truly beautiful possibilities of life, if we simply live a neutral existence."
—Armstrong Williams

AND AT THE END OF THE JOURNEY . . .

Set your compass for the fulfillment of new sensory experiences.

* Life Lesson #2 *

HOW YOU TRAVEL REALLY MATTERS

We travel with intentional spontaneity and passed this trait to our children. Becoming parents in 1985, we knew that we had to share our love of travel with our two daughters. Before they ever started walking, they were already frequent fliers, born with a sense of adventure.

While living in Londonderry, New Hampshire, we drove east to Kennebunkport, Maine, enjoying the beach and walking the coastal town with grandparents in tow. As we drove down State Highway 9, we glanced at a marquee on the Kennebunkport Fire Station building celebrating "Lobster Fest Tonight." Making a quick U-turn, we parked in the lot, walked in, and were escorted to a long wooden table. Ears of golden corn and large red lobsters were dropped in front of each of us by hospitable firemen. We were grinning so hard we could hardly eat. It was an incredible two hours of intentional spontaneity!

No offense to some wonderful hotels found in the United States and around the world, but we choose to stay at places that immerse you into the life of a community. From a camping cabin in Silver Springs, Florida, to a castle with turrets on the Blue Ridge Parkway, we always opted for the off-the-beaten-path lodging. Whether we were visiting the Lower 48 states, the Caribbean, or Europe, we stayed at memorable locations.

In Germany, we stumbled upon a working farm named Gasthof Krone and fortunately found available rooms to spend the night. The owners surprised us with a large breakfast the next morning of fresh milk from their cows, a delightful muesli mix, and fresh tomatoes and cheese. The daughters consider Gasthof Krone to be one of the most memorable places they ever stayed.

Part of intentional spontaneity is arriving to a town and simply asking the locals where they would eat. People are generally gracious and willing to inform visitors of the favorite hangouts. That is how we found the very best barbecue in Memphis, Tennessee, extraordinary cannelloni in Florence, Italy, and the singular most spectacular fish tacos on a hidden beach in Kauai. Now, if only we can repeat that culinary experience back at home.

"The more open you are to wonder, the more of it there will be." —G Adventures

AND AT THE END
OF THE JOURNEY . . .

Travel with
intentional
spontaneity.

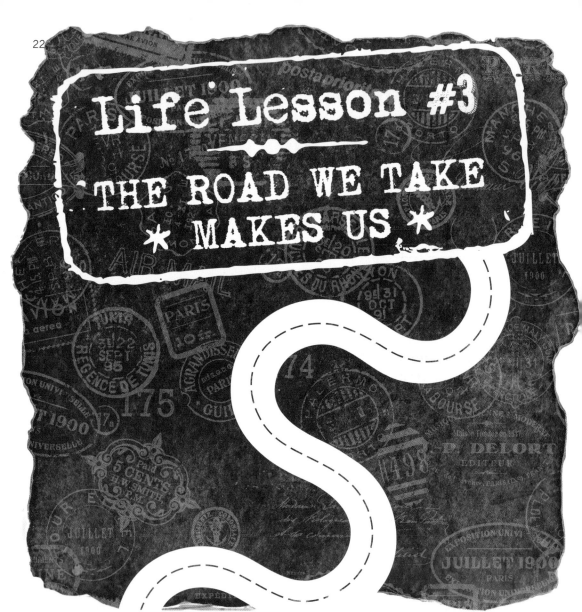

Life Lesson #3

...THE ROAD WE TAKE * MAKES US *

Our daughters spent their most formidable years growing up in Londonderry, New Hampshire. We would take mini family vacations to Derry and visited Robert Frost's farm. It was only seven minutes away. We enjoyed five summers of micro vacations to the historic farm, hunting for frogs, running across fields of wildflowers, and pretending we had found Frost's path that inspired his poem "The Road Not Taken."

In "The Road Not Taken," its beauty lies in that like most poetry, it lends itself to a variety of interpretations. It represents the power and consequence of personal choice and how the outcome of that choice is not revealed until after you have lived with it. It has been and continues to be an inspirational poem, which encourages self-reliance, thinking for yourself, and not following the latest trend.

The Road Not Taken

Two roads diverged in a yellow wood,
And sorry I could not travel both
And be one traveler, long I stood
And looked down one as far as I could
To where it bent in the undergrowth;
Then took the other, as just as fair,
And having perhaps the better claim,
Because it was grassy and wanted wear;
Though as for that the passing there
Had worn them really about the same,
And both that morning equally lay
In leaves no step had trodden black.
Oh, I kept the first for another day!
Yet knowing how way leads on to way,
I doubted if I should ever come back.
I shall be telling this with a sigh
Somewhere ages and ages hence:
Two roads diverged in a wood, and I—
I took the one less traveled by,
And that has made all the difference.

Traveling with family presents a similar microcosm of life choices, whether they are good or bad ones. Somehow we all learn from the small decisions we make, and they have a great impact on our life. Like a family vacation, it is up to us whether we learn from it or not.

"We travel by choice, not to escape life, but for life not to escape us." —Carla Tocquigny

AND AT THE END OF THE JOURNEY . . . .

We know that the road we take makes us, whether it is stone by stone, brick by brick, or already paved for us.

Traveling with family is supposed to be fun, but it often leads to stressful situations.

In the middle of an argument on the beach, we heard a dad yelling at his family, "Dammit, I paid $10,000 for this family vacation so start having fun and stop yelling at each other!"

We dedicate this chapter to families on vacation that have said some pretty funny things.

"It rained the entire vacation and is my father mad! He said some things that people aren't supposed to say." —Max (age five)

"A journey of a thousand miles begins with a cash advance." —Anonymous

"Airplane travel is nature's way of making you look like your passport photo." —Al Gore

"Airline food is the tiniest food I've ever seen in my entire life. Any kind of meat that you get—chicken, steak, anything—has grill marks on each side, like somehow we'll actually believe there's an open-flame grill in the front of the plane." —Ellen DeGeneres

"The worst thing about being a tourist is having other tourists recognize you as a tourist." —Russell Baker

"I told the doctor I broke my leg in two places. He told me to quit going to those places." —Henny Youngman

"Living on earth is expensive, but it does include a free trip around the sun every year." —Petie Tocquigny

"When preparing to travel, lay out all your clothes and all your money. Then take half the clothes and twice the money." —Anonymous

"Thanks to the interstate highway system, it is now possible to travel from coast to coast without seeing anything."
—Charles Kuralt

"My fear of flying starts as soon as I buckle myself in and then the guy up front mumbles a few unintelligible words; then before I know it I'm thrust into the back of my seat by acceleration that seems way too fast and the rest of the trip is an endless nightmare of turbulence, of near misses. And then the cabbie drops me off at the airport." —Dennis Miller

"On a New York subway you get fined for spitting, but you can throw up for nothing." —Lewis Grizzard

"I have found out that there ain't no surer way to find out whether you like people or hate them than to travel with them." —Mark Twain

"We love you, we adore you, but it's hard to be around you."
—Aging mom to daughter on board Holland cruise

"In my parents' 1962 Oldsmobile, I sat perched on the armrest in the front seat, perfectly poised to catapult through the windshield in the event of a wreck. Now my four-year-old is strapped in the back like he's manning a rocket." —Anonymous

"Mom, why isn't there a Mr. Issippi?" —Overheard while crossing America's great river

"Do bipolar people want to see both sides of planet earth on a single family vacation?" —Anonymous

"Some people take dysfunction to lofty heights, especially when they are on a family vacation." —Carla Tocquigny

"I'm going on a three-day getaway, and I've already started packing. I leave in two years for one night." —Jarod Kintz

"A vacation frequently means that the family goes away for a rest, accompanied by a mother who sees that the others get it." —Marcelene Cox

"You can find your way across this country using burger joints the way the early navigators used stars." —Charles Kuralt

"And that's the wonderful thing about family travel: it provides you with experiences that will remain locked forever in the scar tissue of your mind." —Dave Barry

Woman #1 [sitting on the steps of Sacré-Coeur in Paris, perusing brochure of southern Germany and planning the later stages of their trip]: "Do we want to go to this New-swan-stine castle built by this mad king they talk about in here?"
Woman #2: "No, I heard he just copied the one in Disneyland."
—Overheard by Fodor's member

"Everywhere you look, there is nothing but yellow flowers! And if that's all there is, I'M LEAVING!!" —Young woman angrily complaining into a pay phone, overheard by Fodor's member in Death Valley, California, after witnessing a rare display of brilliant wildflowers covering the arid land

"Now, they say that New Zealand is beautiful and I do not know—because after twenty-two hours on a plane any landmass would be beautiful." —Lewis Black

"Can we just live on vacation, Mama?" —Heather (age three)

"When in doubt, go on vacation." —Transformed Traveler journal

"If we were meant to stay in one place, we would have roots instead of feet." —Rachel Wolchin

"I need a six-month vacation, twice a year." —Anonymous

"I love my job only when I'm on vacation." —I Trip

"Seven a.m. on the first day of summer vacation was, to her mind, a dangerous time to be awake. Even God had to be sleeping in." —Victoria Kahler, *Luisa Across the Bay*

"What does it mean to pre-board? Do you get on before you get on?" —George Carlin

AND AT THE END OF THE JOURNEY . . . .

All members of the vacationing family should keep their sense of humor. Your time away from home and together as a family deserves a little levity and laughter.

SECTION TWO
CHANGED PERSPECTIVE

Life Lesson #5

* PRESERVING *
A FABLED VILLAGE

Family vacations can sometimes alter history. Memories of the lovely places you have visited can be held tightly in your heart. For Anna May Snader, she had an opportunity to help preserve the enchanting German fable-like village of Rothenburg.

The second-largest city during the country's Middle Ages, Rothenburg is an experience straight out of the tales from the brothers Grimm complete with a two-mile wall surrounding the city.

Traveling with her family to Rothenburg in the summer of 1915, Anna fell in love with the architecture of forty-two gates and towers. In a general store, she purchased a four-color pencil sketching of the village to grace the walls of her home back in the States.

Nestled in the Tauber River valley, Anna's senses were overwhelmed with the smell of cows, the morning song of meadowlarks, and the taste of local pastry.

The Rothenburg sketch was a constant reminder of how the winds of history can blow through yet hold one small village unchanged. Anna could stand in front of the picture and recall her cherished memories of her family vacation in Germany.

In March 1945, German soldiers were stationed in Rothenburg to defend it. On March 31, sixteen U.S. planes dropped bombs over Rothenburg, killing thirty-seven people and destroying 306 houses, six public buildings, nine watchtowers, and over two thousand feet of the wall encircling the medieval town.

Upon hearing of the escalating bombing by Americans on Germany, Anna May Snader McCloy made a call to Washington, D.C. She was so transfixed by the little fairy-tale village that she commanded her son, U.S. assistant secretary of war John McCloy, to halt the bombing of Rothenburg. She reminded her son of the beautiful sketch of Rothenburg that adorned their living room wall all those many years. She earnestly called upon him to preserve what she held so closely to her heart.

Like a dutiful son, McCloy ordered U.S. Army General Jacob L. Devers to not use artillery in taking Rothenburg. Six soldiers of the Twelfth Infantry Regiment, Fourth Division, were ordered to march into Rothenburg on a three-hour mission and negotiate the surrender of the town. When stopped by a German soldier, Private Lichey, the only American soldier who spoke fluent German, held up a white flag and explained, *"We are representatives of our division commander. We bring you his offer to spare the city of Rothenburg from shelling and bombing if you agree not to defend it. If we haven't returned to our lines by 1800 hours, the town will be bombed and shelled to the ground."* The local military commander, Major Thömmes, gave up the town, ignoring the order of Adolf Hitler for all towns to fight to the end and thereby saving Rothenburg from total destruction by U.S. artillery fire.

American troops of the Twelfth Infantry Regiment, Fourth Division, occupied the town on April 17, 1945, and in November 1948, John McCloy was named honorable protectorate of Rothenburg. After the war, the residents of the city quickly repaired the bombing damage. Donations for rebuilding were received from all over the world. The rebuilt walls now feature commemorative bricks with donor names.

AND AT THE END OF THE JOURNEY . . .

Bring back a piece of your vacation and place it in your home to remember what you loved about your journey.

Life Lesson #6

* OH, THE VIEW IS *
TREMENDOUS

Herschel was a part of a blue-collar family from New Concord, Ohio. Growing up in a modest household, his mom and dad scrimped and saved for family vacations.

It didn't matter where Herschel Sr. and Clara went, their son Herschel ate up every second of the adventure. Legend has it that his dad drove up to one hundred miles per hour and Herschel rolled down his car window, hung his head out the window, and felt his face terrifically blown by the force. His bubble gum blew out of his mouth and his sunglasses were thrust off his face.

Herschel was allowed to climb trees, especially on family vacations. His mom was not the overprotective type and wanted him to grow up without any fears. Seeing the maple trees of New Concord, Herschel would shimmy up the tallest tree for the finest vantage point. There, he could see for miles and view the gently rolling hills, dominated by farms.

On one trip in 1929, Herschel's dad was able to borrow a Waco 10 barnstorming plane and take eight-year-old Herschel for the trip of a lifetime. This was an open-cockpit adventure, with only pilot goggles and a seat belt for protection. Herschel would giggle, saying, *"I couldn't get the view from the air out of my mind."*

Family vacations were great times to learn great life lessons. There were too few family times like this, especially given that the world was at war. Herschel left his precious surroundings of New Concord and joined the U.S. Marine Corps in 1943.

Not surprisingly, from Herschel's past experiences from family vacations, he became a pilot. His inner core values of courage and fearlessness were formed as a kid on idyllic family vacations. Flying fifty-nine missions during World War II and ninety during the Korean War were not just a part of his duty, but a natural course that began as a boy on the road with his family.

For Herschel's 149 missions during two wars, he received the Distinguished Flying Cross six times. In 1954, he was chosen as a test pilot for a top secret initiative. In 1957, Herschel flew in "Project Bullet" and set the speed record by flying from Los Angeles to New York in three hours and twenty-three minutes.

John "Herschel" Glenn became one of America's first astronauts and the first man to orbit the earth, 162 miles above New Concord, Ohio. On February 20, 1962, his space capsule, *Friendship 7*, was launched from Cape Canaveral, Florida, and made three orbits before landing in the Atlantic Ocean near the Bahamas. Echoing the past voice of Herschel, John told the world, "Oh, that view is tremendous."

His parents would have been proud. John's ride into space helped America catch up in the space race with Russia. He was given a hero's welcome for conquering the gravity of Earth and lifting America's spirit of adventure.

"Dad was my hero. He wanted to give the curiosity and sense of unbounded possibility that could come from learning." —John Glenn

AND AT THE END OF THE JOURNEY . . .

Give your children the opportunity to climb high, get a great view, run fast, feel the wind in their face, and have a sense of fearlessness.

Life Lesson #7

PROTECT WHAT YOU
* LOVE *

Jack's love for the ocean, nature, and traveling inspired him to join the French Navy in 1930. In 1935, he was in a car accident, broke his back, and was unable to use his arms. Doctors told him to go swim in the Mediterranean Ocean to rebuild his strength. Jack eventually regained mobility, but his career in naval aviation came to an end, turning his attention underwater.

Captain Philippe Tailliez gave Jack a pair of underwater goggles that launched his life of curiosity and innovation, building devices to explore the undersea world. During the 1940s, Jack improved the Aqua-Lung design, which led to the invention of scuba.

Later, he founded French Oceanographic Campaigns (FOC) and, for a symbolic single franc, he leased a ship called *Calypso* from Thomas Guinness. *Calypso*, a former minesweeper, became his research vessel. *Calypso*'s maiden voyage was in 1950, when Jack went to the Red Sea to study coral reefs. Jack also launched his adventure as a parent.

As a young boy, son Philippe remembered his father Jack, donning his little red hat and charming grin, telling him, "Il faut aller voir," or "We must go and see for ourselves." It's a principle that stuck with

Philippe throughout his relatively short life. Despite his dad's fame, few people know that "go and see for yourself" was the family's philosophy while on vacation and certainly for life itself.

Philippe recalled that family vacations often blended into filmmaking. Using Dad's underwater camera, they filmed sleeping sharks near the Yucatan coast of Mexico, extraordinary sea life near Portugal's Azores Islands, and unseen parts of the Antarctic region.

"Dad's singular priority, and lifelong love, was the ocean. That's why his legacy as an adventuring father is legendary." He was, indeed, the man who opened our eyes to what happens underneath the boat.

He was a great advocate for the sea, and also for family travel. By taking family vacations with his children, Jack imparted wisdom about the earth's oceans, rhythms, and value to man's very existence. He believed that people protect what they love; for him, it was the sea. He said, "From birth, man carries the weight of gravity on his shoulders. He is bolted to earth. But man has only to sink beneath the surface and he is free."

As a public figure, Jack (Jacques-Yves) Cousteau continued to actively protect the ocean. He organized a publicity campaign, and stopped a train, carrying waste to the sea, on its tracks, with the help of women and children. To help protect the ocean, he founded the Cousteau Society in 1973, which is still a large and thriving organization. And the flaming torch of passion for the sea has been passed on to a fourth generation of Cousteaus who believe that "only the impossible missions are those that succeed."

"If a man, for whatever reason, has the opportunity to lead an extraordinary life, he has no right to keep it to himself."
—Jacques Cousteau

AND AT THE END OF THE JOURNEY . . .

Impart wisdom as you travel with your children.

Life Lesson #8

STAYING ALIVE

The Von Trapp family did it, George Clooney did it, and so did the Bee Gees.

Families will travel to a place and find it so enchanting that they decide to move there. When the Von Trapp family visited Stowe, Vermont, there was something so familiar about the place. The roaming hills, the fresh air, the friendly townspeople. It seemed like Salzburg, Austria, to them and they made their home there.

Over twenty years ago, George Clooney vacationed with his extended family to northern Italy. He was so mesmerized by the area, the food, and the ambiance that he made Lake Como a permanent part of his life with a home.

In the early 1970s, the popular family singing trio, the brothers Gibb, formally known as the Bee Gees, had hit the wall of creativity. Following a line of great hits from 1966 to 1968 with "Massachusetts," "I Gotta Get a Message to You," and "Smile," the brothers were searching for a new sound.

On a family vacation to Miami in 1971, Barry, Maurice, and Robin were caught up in the sensations of South Florida. Perhaps it was the fusion of Cuban, Puerto Rican, and Floridian culture that overwhelmed their ears, eyes, and taste buds. They loved the area so much and regained their songwriting momentum.

Inspired by their new local surroundings, their new digs and renewed sense of purpose led them to write the songs that defined the 1970s disco scene. Robert Stigwood, producer for *Saturday Night Fever*, called their agent and asked them to write the songs for the movie. "Staying Alive" became the anthem for an entire new generation. "How Deep Is Your Love" ranks as one of the greatest love songs ever written . . . all influenced by a family vacation that truly moved the participants.

AND AT THE END OF THE JOURNEY . . .

Family vacations may lead to a new place to live.

Life Lesson #9

TRAVEL INSPIRES DESIGN

"And the winner is Scheme #218." It was the culmination of much travel, especially family vacations, that exposed a budding architect to the nautical world.

Danish-born Jorn arrived into this world on April 9, 1918. His dad was the director of a shipyard in Copenhagen, Denmark. Jorn was blessed with family travel that included holidays aboard sailing vessels. Adventuring in the Baltic and Mediterranean Seas, Jorn and his dad visited shipyards, witnessing the design and construction of great sailing vessels. Someday, Jorn would turn his objects of affection into his architectural legacy.

Jorn's dad was an enthusiastic mariner and urged him to become a naval engineer. Instead, Jorn opted to study architecture at the Royal Danish Academy of Fine Arts. Over the next decade, he practiced his craft but used travel to formulate his philosophy. He visited Morocco, China, Japan, India, and Australia, the latter destined to become a major factor in his life.

Graduating in 1942 from the academy with a degree in architecture, Jorn initially found work in Finland. Seven years later, he and his wife, Lis, traveled to the United States and Mexico on an educational grant. **Being introduced to Frank Lloyd Wright and other industry visionaries influenced his sense of form and beauty.**

Between 1950 and 1956, Jorn established his own architectural practice in Copenhagen. He and Lis continued to travel extensively, stretching his imagination. He was so stimulated by travel and sailing that his designs transcended into the form of buildings. Passion and design were inseparable.

Entering an international design competition in 1956, Jorn was intrigued by the idea of designing an entertainment theater for the performing arts, especially at Bennelong Point, Australia. Once a small island connected to the land at low tide, it had two large middens. Jorn found out that Aboriginal people used it as a place for ceremony and feasting.

Four judges, including Eero Saarinen, reviewed over two hundred entries. Jorn's rendition stopped the judges in their tracks. Were Eero and his colleagues seeking a design or an iconic statement that would define a country's look?

On January 29, 1957, the thirty-eight-year-old Dane, Jorn Utzon, was declared the winner of the Sydney Opera House design competition. Embedded in its form were the sails and hulls of a distant vessel, once seen in his childhood and now manifested in one of the most celebrated buildings of our time.

"It stands by itself as one of the indisputable masterpieces of human creativity, not only in the 20th century but in the history of humankind." —UNESCO World Heritage Committee, 2007

AND AT THE END
OF THE JOURNEY . . .

Family vacations can have a lasting impact, especially on the imaginative minds of our children.

Life Lesson #10

WE ARE THE
POOR ONES

A very wealthy, well-to-do father took his son and daughter on a family vacation for the specific purpose of showing them how poor people live.

Together, they spent a couple of nights on a farm with a family in Central America.

As they returned to the comforts of their luxurious home, the father asked, "How was the trip? Did you see how poor people live?" "Oh, yeah," said the daughter. "So tell me, what did you learn from this trip?" the father wanted to know.

"I saw that we have one dog and they have five, plus a cat. We have this pool that reaches to the middle of our yard. They have a creek that seemed endless.

"We decorate around our pool with imported lanterns. They have the stars at night. And our patio reaches out twenty feet to the property line. They have the whole horizon. We have this small piece of land, and they have fields that went far beyond my sight.

"We have servants to serve us, but they served others.

"We buy our expensive, organic food, and they grow their own fresh vegetables.

"We live in a gated community with security cars and closed-circuit cameras monitoring every movement. They have friends to protect them."

The father was speechless. The daughter concluded with, "Thank you for showing me how poor we are."

Travel can be the most clarifying experience. We are often absent of the most important things in life that money simply can't buy.

"He who is contented is rich." —Lao-tzu

AND AT THE END OF THE JOURNEY . . .

The absence of material things often changes perspective.

Life Lesson #11

* JOURNAL *
YOUR ADVENTURE

"The traveler who stays long . . . seems to produce a good story." —Ted Conover

With great anticipation, Nick's family started packing for their big family vacation. On this trip, they would embark on the great trading trail to India. Nick's children had not spent much time with their dad as he was a frequent, international traveler. All that his children knew was that he was connected with local government and friends of high officials within the Catholic Church.

Dad chose an interesting route for this particular trip. As a fifteen-year-old, his son Marc had never experienced life outside of Italy. He was anxious to see special port cities like Acre, just outside of Jerusalem.

Instead of risking a sea passage to India and the Far East, Nick proceeded with his family over land. Traveling through arid deserts toward eastern Iran, they reached Afghanistan. One of Marc's brothers fell ill with malaria, and the family was forced to stay in this seemingly friendly country until he was well enough to travel.

Marc viewed the world through a wide-angle lens. He saw the North Star as appearing to dip below the horizon. One day he would write about the extraordinary people that he met along the thirty-six-month journey across Siberia and Mongolia to the land known as Cathay.

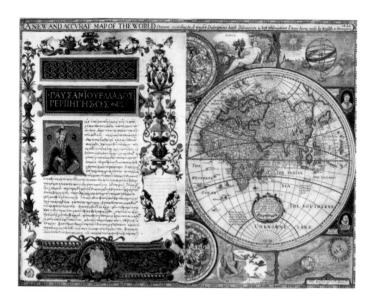

Marc absorbed the sights and smells of the Middle East. His account of the Orient, especially, provided the Western world with its first clear picture of the East's geography and ethnic customs.

Upon arrival to Cathay, Marc learned firsthand of his dad's relationship with the monarchy led by Kublai Khan. In previous trips, Nick had instructed the Khan family in the traditions and customs of Venice. When they returned to the Peking Palace, they welcomed Nick and his sons with open arms.

Over the next six years, Marc became fluent in the Chinese language, earning the deep trust of the monarchy. Marc was afforded the opportunity to serve as a governor over a city and was granted special envoy privileges from the monarchy, representing a modern-day passport to any part of the country.

Upon Marc's return to Venice, he became involved in the war against Genoa, captaining one of the naval ships. Captured and imprisoned by the Genoan leadership, Marc lost his freedom and nobility that he had once cherished from Cathay. Befriending a fellow prisoner named Rustichello, Marc shared his illustrious travels with his new friend, who romantically wrote the stories in longhand.

They titled his travel chronicles, written in French, as *Books of the Marvels of the World*. For Marc, known as Marco Polo, inspired countless travelers with the factual accounts of traveling from Venice to Cathay. Future explorers, like Christopher Columbus, carried *The Travels of Marco Polo* as a companion to guide their own adventures.

As the original transformed traveler, Marco Polo's lessons from extended family adventures were many:

- There is a direct correlation of advanced learning with traveling outside of your comfort zone. Marco was a quick study as he discovered the Silk Route to the East with his dad.
- Keep a journal from all of your family vacations, whether they last seven days or seven months. Marco wrote his own story from details he recorded.
- Study other cultures and learn a foreign language. Marco could speak four languages and won the confidence of Kublai Khan.

- Be transformed by food and bring it back to your home. Marco brought back noodles from China to Venice—and the rest is history.
- Who you know matters! Khan gave Marco a golden tablet that gave him access to any part of China. He was always backed up by royalty.
- Be engaged with locals in cultural events. Fully immersed travelers are very endearing. Marco stayed in China for seventeen years and became a friend to many.
- Share all of your tales. On his deathbed, Marco told a priest that Europe had only heard half of his adventures.

AND AT THE END OF THE JOURNEY . . .

Write down your adventure and share it with the world.

Life Lesson #12

* THE ACE *
NEGOTIATOR

"Don't lose perspective." —Anonymous

No street merchant was going to get the better of me. No way. I'd read the Frommer's guidebooks. I knew I wasn't supposed to pay full sticker price for anything, especially in Brazil.

We were in Salvador, Brazil, a lovely port city with an impressive heritage. Admiring narrow boulevards, old fishermen, and the multicolored houses, we headed to the public market. **Like many other markets, it was sensory overload with wafting food odors, spices, and the typical array of local arts and crafts.**

I got my heart set on purchasing a locally made percussion instrument. Double cowbells. Two unique tones. Perfect for our band's rendition of "Black Magic Woman."

I picked out my silver cowbells, welded in a U shape, and walked them over to the girl in charge. In my broken Portuguese, I asked how much. She quoted me a price. I sized her up and made a counteroffer. She paused to calculate and made a counter-counteroffer. Back and forth. Her price, my price, her price, my price. Always edging closer to each other.

Finally, making a stand, I held my price. I reached in my pocket, took out my money, counted out the exact amount of my offer, and held it out to her. This was it. The decisive moment. She accepted and I got a great new sound for the band.

As I walked away with my prized cowbells, victorious as a world-class negotiator, I heard our youngest daughter say, "Congratulations, you just spent ten minutes bargaining fifty cents out of a teenage girl in Brazil." I went back and gave the girl all the change in my pocket.

AND AT THE END OF THE JOURNEY . . .

Bargain with a giving heart.

Life Lesson #13

* ELEPHANTS *
STOOD VIGIL

"By choice, we have become a family, first in our hearts, and finally in breath and being. Great expectations are good; great experiences are better." —Richard Fischer

We came to know Lawrence through our family travels to Africa.

In 1999, this South African wildlife conservationist received a call from an organization asking him if he had room for a herd of nine elephants on his reserve centered in KwaZulu-Natal.

Traumatized by poachers, these erratic teenager elephants would be shot if Lawrence did not adopt them. He was the last resort.

As an "elephant whisperer," Lawrence built trust by the tone of his voice. Nana, one of the strongest-willed elephants, always broke out of camp. On one particular warm day, she put her trunk through the fence toward Lawrence. As if to signal a turning point, Nana indicated that she wanted to touch Lawrence.

After that incident, Lawrence released the herd into the broader expanses of his reserve. There they wandered, foraged, and reproduced into a sizable community. But they made Lawrence a part of that family. Surprisingly, every time that Lawrence would travel, the herd would return to their original compound at KwaZulu-Natal to welcome him back from his adventures. The herd traveled over fifty miles to make this trek and welcome their friend.

Years later, we learned that Lawrence was called into Baghdad Zoo to save the beloved animals in the midst of the U.S.-led invasion of Iraq. By the time he arrived, only thirty-five of the 650 animals were found alive. With the aid of community volunteers, Lawrence rescued the remaining animals known as "Babylon's Ark."

Sadly, Lawrence Anthony suffered a fatal heart attack while on a trip to Johannesburg, four hundred miles away from his reserve. When his body was returned, the adopted elephant herd stood vigil outside the gates of the compound. Not having been seen for six months, they had returned, and they mourned their beloved friend for many hours before turning back into the outer reaches of the reserve.

AND AT THE END
OF THE JOURNEY . . .

Expect the world
community to
adopt you.

Life Lesson #14
DISPONIBLE

As we traveled through the poverty-stricken Appalachian Mountains in the 1960s, my parents taught us to be open to the pains and pleasures of others. Papa Tocquigny, with his strongest French accent, would call it *disponible*. Dad would call it openness, emotional availability, and willingness to shed a tear for others.

We traveled into the backwoods, where shanties and lean-to structures were common. There was no sign of running water or electricity, much less shoes. Our hand-me-down clothes from older cousins seemed luxurious.

Dad saw an old-time peddler on a wagon led by three mules. The entire family stopped to listen to the conversation between white-bearded Jack Ratliff and my dad.

Jack shared the story of his own plight and poverty in the happiest manner. He had been evicted from his home and had adapted to the road. Living off animals he trapped and an occasional handout from strangers, this happy wanderer was trekking across the hills meeting all sorts of tourists.

Dressed in muddy Levi denims with a red checkered shirt, Jack sported a rustic hat to cover his bald head. He introduced us to his three traveling companions—a rat terrier named Village, a white billy goat referred to as Buster, and a very red hen named Iris. His companions sat on the mules for our Kodak moment.

Jack taught us a valuable lesson that day about poverty and self-esteem. He told us that one of the reasons inequality gets so deep in this country is that everyone wants to be rich. That's the American ideal. Poor people don't like talking about poverty, because even though they might live in a shack in the Smoky Mountains or in a wagon like his, they don't consider themselves to be poor.

Jack was not poor in his own eyes and didn't want to be treated as such. He was thankful for the shirt on his back, the food that was provided, and the opportunity to meet new friends.

His destitute story about the loss of his wife and kids made Mom shed a tear. She gave each of us a coin to share with Mr. Ratliff and also handed him a few dollars. Back in 1965, $5.75 was a lot of money, especially to Mom.

"In poverty and other misfortunes of life, true friends are a sure refuge." —Aristotle

AND AT THE END OF THE JOURNEY . . .

Embrace the travails and pains of those less fortunate than you.

While our family was vacationing in Africa, we heard the legendary story about when Dr. David Livingstone met Mr. Henry Morton Stanley, a news reporter. Stanley loved to report about Livingstone's encounters with wildlife, but he might have missed one of the great lessons.
As told to us by our guide Ben, one day Livingstone was attacked by a male lion. The lion was about to make his fatal bite into Livingstone's neck before a nearby hunter gunned down the creature. Years later, when Stanley asked him how he felt, Livingstone replied that when he realized there was virtually nothing he could do in the midst of a lion attack, his terror went to a peaceful calm. He had reached a peacefulness that transcended any previous feeling.

Was it Livingstone's resignation to die? "If this is how I'm going down, then let it happen."

As Ben explained, in the clutches of death, the good doctor utterly released himself from life, breaking all the chains of the past. He urged us to travel like Dr. Livingstone, wholly being in the present moment, letting go of all the pressures of life, and acting fully alive. He also emphasized that his tour did not include close encounters with lions that would teach us lessons!

"If you want to identify me, ask me not where I live, or what I like to eat, but ask me what I am living for, in detail, and ask me what I think is keeping me from living fully for the thing I want to live for." —Thomas Merton

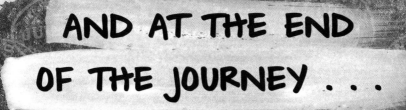

AND AT THE END
OF THE JOURNEY . . .

Let yourself go
from all of life's
pressures.

SECTION THREE
SENSORY TRAVEL

Life Lesson #16

IT'S SO COMMON
SENSORY

"Sink into the peacefulness of the place you have discovered through travel." —Petie Tocquigny

Starting in 1964, our families took vacations through our five senses. The people we met, the sights and sounds, flavors and fragrances we experienced created the most lasting memories.

Mom used to say that the first taste of something new is always the best. To that end, we experienced unique regional food at street fairs and restaurants along Route 66 as though we were visitors from a foreign country. We really paid attention to how it looked on the plate, the initial appetizing smell, and, of course, the initial taste to our buds. With great awareness in every bite, Mom would ask, "How many distinct details can you detect in every spoonful?"

Mom and Dad also paid attention to the sounds of every place we visited. They would ask, "What did you hear in that little town?" Often, it was simply the hypnotic sound of cicadas, the laughter of children, a marching band, the sound of a passing train, or an old man whistling. Why on earth would God give you two ears and only one mouth? Mathematically, it made sense to listen deeply with the two-to-one ratio. As Mom said, if you aren't listening, you aren't fully experiencing this place!

Through family vacations, our eyes were opened to the many wonders of travel. We were taught to focus on the unordinary and shift our awareness away from the mundane. That's why we visited almost every botanical garden in America in search of the most beautiful, fragrant Tropicana rose. Our old vacation albums have more pictures of roses than us kids!

"Reflect on the journey and celebrate each step of the adventure." —Petie Tocquigny

AND AT THE END OF THE JOURNEY . . .

Pay attention to
every sensory detail.

* Life Lesson #17 *

CARRY A SENSE OF HOME WITH YOU

HOME
sweet
HOME

During our first family vacations as young children, Mom eased us into the art of travel by bringing a few comforts of home along with us. In her arsenal was a washrag for Dad, Dennis's favorite pillow, our familiar bar of soap, and even a sachet of lavender in her suitcase.

Mom had a sense about our own five senses. She knew that the smell of cinnamon made us happy, a cool washrag made Dad more civilized, and a well-rested family was happier for the long, hot road ahead.

Mom made family vacations adventurous travel into strange new places, while keeping the familiar near at hand. She helped us achieve authentic discovery by staying connected to a few small details, increasing our overall vacation enjoyment.

We have heard from other moms and dads on their mastery of this. . . .

"Pack lightly and maintain a sense of home while on vacation. It will make your return a little bit sweeter." —Petie Tocquigny

AND AT THE END OF THE JOURNEY . . .

Carry a little bit of home with you.

Life Lesson #18

MUSIC TO OUR EARS

We travel to delight our ears. You should plan your family vacations for a sensory experience, especially when it comes to treating your ears. Here are some of our favorites:

- Brooklyn Tabernacle Choir, Brooklyn, New York, fills our ears with inspiration.
- Vernazza, Italy, is the home of many angelic voices singing "Ave Maria," often when all the lights of this Cinque Terre village are dimmed for candlelight.
- San Andres and La Mesa, Mexico, are home to millions of monarch butterflies. Listen to the soft roar of fluttering every October.
- The Keys in South Florida are often defined by the sound of sea life, including the most fun loving, rapid talking dolphins on this planet.

- Seek out waterfalls to hear the sound of rushing torrents at Niagara Falls, New York and Ontario; Rainbow Falls, Hawaii; Gozalandia, San Sebastian, Puerto Rico; Victoria Falls, Zambia; Multnomah Falls, Portland, Oregon; and Yosemite Falls, Yosemite National Park, California.

AND AT THE END OF THE JOURNEY . . .

Create lasting memories around the exquisite sounds from your family vacation.

Life Lesson #19

* MEETING * NEW PEOPLE

"MOON RIVER"

While traveling as a family, our daughters, Heather and Jennifer, discovered the lost art of interesting, animated, face-to-face conversation. While the people of Savannah, Georgia, have not cornered the market on this art, greeting people there was like seeing friends that you've known all your life.

Nancy Mercer, song lyricist Johnny Mercer's ("Moon River," "Days of Wine and Roses," "Hooray for Hollywood") niece, had cultivated a peaceful, graceful manner for all who met her. At the local ice cream parlor in downtown Savannah, Nancy took one-on-one conversation to a new height and drew out profound commentary from our daughters:

- Unplug from your digital world and connect personally.
- Drop ranks and become a part of the community.
- When your burdens of work are put aside, your mind is free to capture the pureness of great company.
- Seek out the true nature of people through conversation.
- Everything that you see with your eyes, hear with your ears, all different encounters are perspective shapers for your mind.

- Meeting new people may be the greatest leadership course.
- Get enlightened for the sake of others, not yourself.
- Forget about yourself and just go about wandering.
- Wish happiness and peace upon everyone you meet.
- Before you speak, consider your tone, kindness, your loudness, and if silence may be a better option.
- Listen to the stories of new friends. Never interrupt, just tune in.

"Walk the earth as if your feet were kissing the ground in front of the person you are about to encounter." —Nancy Mercer

AND AT THE END OF THE JOURNEY . . .

Find pure enjoyment from face-to-face conversation with a new friend.

Life Lesson #20

AWAKEN YOUR NOSE

"To inhale is to capture, to experience!" —C. JoyBell

Most travelers miss opportunities to awaken their noses and take in great fragrances while on family vacation. Our favorites include the following:
- We love Mack's Apple Farm, during harvest season in Londonderry, New Hampshire.
- Fragonard Perfumery in Eze, France, opened our noses to the intersection of rose, lemon, mandarin, sage, and amber.
- No plant expresses the grace of the South better than gardenia. Intensely fragrant white blossoms contrast beautifully with shiny, leathery dark green leaves. Take a trip to Birmingham or Tuscaloosa, Alabama, to smell them in full bloom around April.

- Visit Kennewick, Washington, in June and get a whiff of the largest crop of spearmint and peppermint. When you chew Wrigley's gum, you are chewing a part of Kennewick.
- Fresh-baked bread is prepared every morning across the world. Aromaz is a little bakery run by the folks that own Dragon Dynasty that's in the Chartwell mall and they have truly outstanding Char Siu buns, as well as tiny macaroon-coconut tarts, egg tarts, and cream-filled coconut buns.
- For a variety of spices, visit two of our favorite open markets, Marrakesh in Morocco and the souks at the Grand Bazaar in Istanbul, Turkey, that features over three thousand vendors on sixty-one covered streets. Your nose will never get over this experience!
- A favorite destination for both coffee and seafood goes to Pike Place in Seattle, Washington. It's not about Starbucks, but about the passion that all coffee shop owners have as artisans of their trade.

AND AT THE END OF THE JOURNEY . . .

Plan your trips around fragrances.

Life Lesson #21

PANAMA HATS . . . MADE WITH PRIDE

"Every day's an adventure when I step out of my door. That's why I usually wear a hat." —Steve Buscemi

Traveling to Montecristi, Ecuador with friends Ken and Rosalie Asarch, we were in search of the perfect jipijapa . . . a Panama hat. Not that long ago, Spanish merchant Manuel Alfaro realized the hat's potential to meet the needs of foreigners.

Manuel began to export Montecristis, also known as jipijapas, to California for gold rush workers in the mid-1840s. His son, Eloy Alfaro, expanded the export business and eventually rose to be president of Ecuador, financing his liberal revolution through hats.

The building of the Panama Canal in 1904 brought Teddy Roosevelt's and the world media's attention to the Montecristi. Teddy's display of the hat solidified the name "Panama hat" forever in the minds of American men . . . but the real, authentic hats came from Ecuador!

Creating a *jipijapa*, or Panama hat, is not easy. We were fortunate enough to find a Montecristi shop owned by a three-generation family. The grandmother welcomed us into their home modestly equipped with one sink, sparse lighting, and a few chairs. She introduced us to her daughter, who was separating the sheaths of *cogollos*.

Enjoying this sensory experience, the grandmother showed us how she worked the *cogollos* through her nimble fingers.

On any given day in the spring, the family weaves at dawn or late in the evening so the hot sun will not dry up their precious raw material. Watching the family at work, the mother, humped over, starts by creating a rosette, the center of the crown, using eight fibers in a very tight lattice. As she proceeds, new *cogollos* are added to increase the size of the crown. Once completed, the artisan places the form on a tripod stand where she can work from a more upright posture. This standing position gives Mother a better look at making the perfect brim. The fine quality of each hat can be measured by the number of rows in each crown. The tighter the weave, the higher the quality. This painstaking process can take up to a month depending on the artisan's level of exquisite detail.

To the buyers of their product, they own an authentic Panama hat from Montecristi, elegantly handmade from Ecuador.

AND AT THE END OF THE JOURNEY . . .

Try on the family-made products during your travels. You may wear it well.

Life Lesson #22

THE CHILDLIKE FEELING OF REVERENCE

One can travel the world and observe different beliefs all through the eyes of a child. By adventuring out to personally experience the world's religious events, our appreciation for what is beautiful and good in human life has grown immeasurably.

- Christmas in Bethlehem recalls Jesus's birth with expected authenticity.
- Performed every ten years, The Passion Play in Oberammergau, Germany, celebrates Christ's life, crucifixion, and resurrection.
- The Diwali, festival of lights in India, draws millions of Hindus.
- The month of Ramadan in Egypt is an extraordinary event of fasting and prayer within the Islamic faith.
- The Day of Vesak (across Southeast Asia) celebrates the birth, enlightenment, and death of Siddhartha Gautama, known as Buddha.

- Originally derided by all the U.S.-based scientists and men of faith, Yanomami shamans in South America's Amazon region use hundreds of different plants to treat AIDS, cancer, malaria, and even earaches. Nature's pharmacy creates its own religious experience.
- Feeding homeless people in Boulder, Colorado, at Thanksgiving helps one to see all people as God sees them.

"Travel leads to respect for mankind." —Rick Tocquigny

AND AT THE END OF THE JOURNEY . . .

Travel illuminates and leaves you with a childlike feeling of reverence.

Life Lesson #23

STUMBLING UPON HAPPINESS

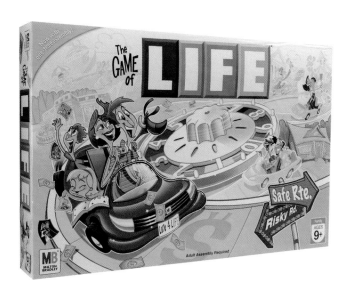

Brothers Tom, seven years young, and Timothy, five, were on a trip to Florida with their mom and dad. Their adventure included two days at Magic Kingdom, SeaWorld, visiting Harry Potter at Universal Studios, and even a trip to Cape Canaveral to fuel their interest as future astronauts.

The brothers had anxiously awaited this special trip for the last eighteen months. Money had been tight since Dad lost his job. The family made it through their tough valley with both Mom and Dad taking multiple jobs to make ends meet.

Now that Dad was gainfully employed again, the family had a renewed energy and stood ready for a special family vacation, especially to celebrate Dad's success.

On the third night of the family vacation, central Florida was bombarded by a weather front that featured a dramatic lightning show and accompanied symphony of thunder. In one flash, the power went out, leaving the family of four in a pitch-black room.

Fortunately, Mom had brought a tiny travel candle, and the boys had packed their miniature flashlights. Now disconnected from the rest of the world, the family decided to play old-fashioned games that Mom and Dad remembered from their childhood. Tom and Timothy got the biggest laughs from this special game time in the dark.

Upon their return Tim asked his dad a very important question. "Dad, we loved the time on vacation when the lights went out so much. Can we have a power outage night?" So Mom and Dad started "Power Outage Night," and it became the one night of the week for family games and total digital disconnect.

Our happiest moments always seem to come when we stumble upon them, and they are often free.

"Our longings are to some degree overblown, because we have within us the capacity to manufacture the very commodity we are constantly chasing when we choose experience." —Dan Gilbert

AND AT THE END OF THE JOURNEY . . .

Bring home a new tradition that you created while on your family vacation.

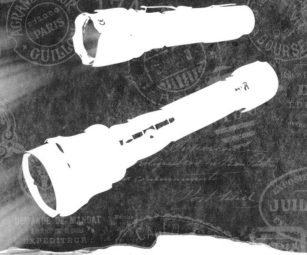

SECTION FOUR
TRAVEL COMPANIONS

Life Lesson #24
* SPENT *

SPENT: /'spent/ adjective (ME, fr. to spend) 15th century *1. used up: CONSUMED. 2. exhausted of active components or qualities used for a particular purpose. 3. drained of energy or effectiveness. 4. state reached at end of family vacation.*

To most travelers, family vacations are precious moments spent with loved ones. But for over fifty million Americans, family vacation also means going out to serve others through volunteering and coming home "spent"—physically and emotionally exhausted—in a good way.

For John and Chrys Howard, and their children and grandchildren (of *Duck Dynasty* fame), going on mission trips connects them to other cultures in a powerful way, reminding them of our shared humanity. Their unique approach to travel is about sharing their time, talent, and resources to preserve the character of the place they visit and to make a difference. For their offspring, they have discovered that mission trips may be physically exhausting, but singularly the most memorable. One summer, the family was blessed to go from the luxury of a cruise vacation to the interior of poverty-stricken Dominican Republic. All family members agree that the Dominican Republic trip was more significant and life shaping.

John and Chrys's global perspective was shaped by two things. One was attending four different Olympic Games: Montreal, Los Angeles, Atlanta, and Salt Lake City. There they saw the world's finest athletes trained for their one moment in time. Cutting across cultural and political differences, their family applauded every athlete from EVERY country. **Spending time in the Olympic Villages, their children saw firsthand how the entire world could intersect for one purpose—experiencing global togetherness.**

Another important piece of the mission-minded puzzle involved John's dad, Alton Howard. Alton was a successful entrepreneur who came from humble beginnings. He was quick to see the need for relief to people struggling all around the world. In 1981, when Poland was released from the grips of Communism, Alton was instrumental in organizing efforts to take food to the country and disperse to those in need. John was one of the drivers on that mission effort, while Alton worked at home to raise the necessary funds. From that effort, a relief ministry was formed, which the family has been privileged to support both physically and financially.

The Howards have shared meals and experiences with volunteers serving rural groups in Africa, Romania, the Dominican Republic, Mexico, Brazil, and Haiti. Chrys calls their mission-minded travel *"connection vacations."* "John and I love being able to share and learn from people from all around the world. We love to see inside the world of other cultures and give our children and grandchildren a deeper understanding of life while helping to improve the lives of the people we visit. Connecting with people around the world builds our connection with our family members too."

The Howards' hands-on experiences have provided them a journey filled with service projects that truly mattered, opportunities to share their personal faith, and a closer look at the direct impact of their volunteer service. In retrospect,

"our children learned to be givers versus receivers."

"It's not about us and keeping record of all the good deeds performed, it's about putting others first and serving." From building houses and improving water systems to creating eco-friendly communities, mission-oriented family vacations can be life altering.

"I think every family should go on at least one mission effort as a family. We've sent our kids on trips and that's great, too, but it's very meaningful to experience it together. You will all gain a greater appreciation for what we have in America and make memories that will last a lifetime," Chrys adds.

You, too, can transform your family vacation into a "connection trip" and become advocates for a country, immersing yourselves in culture and service.

"Staying young is the best state of mind."
—John F. Kennedy

AND AT THE END OF THE JOURNEY . . .

Helping others can bind a family together.

Life Lesson #25

* STAYING *
YOUTHFUL

Getting older is inevitable, but choosing to take family vacations with your kids, regardless of age, is optional. Growing older physically is something we all do, but putting off travel with family is a mistake.

John Wessel recently had the opportunity to take his eighty-five-year-old father, Ralph, on a trip to visit his cousin Joe Collins in Santa Cruz, California. It seemed that disappearing, stopping unexpectedly, or sometimes just veering off into the unknown is the norm when traveling with Ralph. Could it be that it's because Dad is tired, bored, or just curious?

Ralph loves to talk to strangers. He is attracted to people who are behind desks. Ralph is like the boys who run a stick up against a fence, teasing the dog barking on the other side. Other times he believes it is HIS job to talk to people.

One morning John, his son, and his dad took a drive to the Monterey Bay Aquarium. This is a beautiful museum located right on the ocean and known for its penguins. What is the one thing that John's dad remembers about the aquarium? The penguins have the ability to "projectile poop" up to six feet!

The aquarium has a children's touching area, but before you enter, you pass through a "look and see" area. Ralph walked over to the pool and immediately read the sign that says, "Do not put your hands in the water." Just like a kid, he dove his hand right into the water. John almost put him in time-out.

John proceeded to lead his own child into the "touch and feel" area. The two volunteers behind the counter provided detail on the creatures. With instructions to "touch softly," Curious Ralph started prodding this sea creature with his fingers. Blame it on his hearing.

It can be challenging for Linda Fodrini-Johnson of Walnut Creek, California, to find a mutually agreeable summer vacation spot with her eighty-eight-year-old mother, who no longer likes beaches or hot weather. One summer, Ms. Fodrini-Johnson, who is the founder and executive director of Eldercare Services and past president of the National Association of Professional Geriatric Care Managers, rented a cabin in the Sierras.

"My mother can sit on a beautiful deck and enjoy the forest and watch the wildlife, and she'll sit in the shade in a beach chair while I swim," she said. "Just being in the mountains is renewing for her."

Getting up out of your familiar bed in the morning, making those sounds of being old, will put you on a path to grow old before your time. Vacations, particularly with family, break the usual pattern of life. You grow older faster by staying in the same surroundings.

"Grow old with me and take family vacations until you are ninety-three" is the new mantra. The lesson of travel is that adventure keeps you young. **Go travel and meet new people, taste new foods, hear new sounds, smell new fragrances, and see new sights.** It's an opportunity to react to stimuli, whether it's your family or the surroundings. You will keep a fresh view of the world, perhaps acting a little rambunctious and youthfully silly!

"Staying young is the best state of mind." —Rick Tocquigny

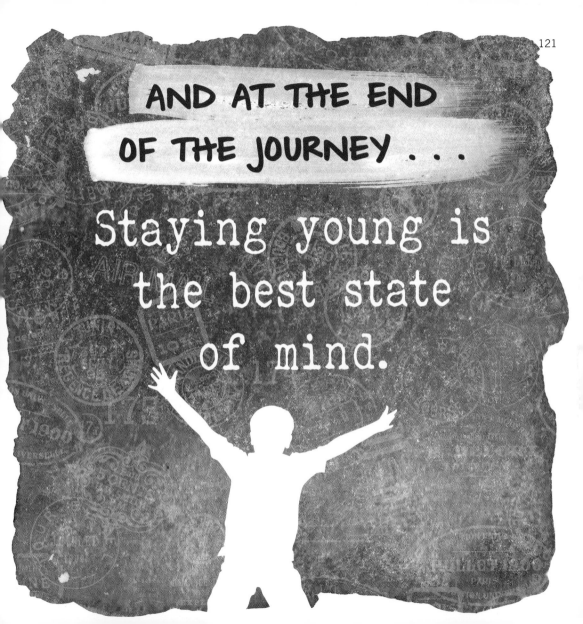

AND AT THE END OF THE JOURNEY . . .

Staying young is the best state of mind.

Life Lesson #26

This Is a Test, Only a Test

"Sometimes, they don't know what's best for them, like a good ole fashioned road trip." —George J. Tocquigny

The civil defense warnings in the 1960s urged us to take shelter for possible Communist missile strikes on the United States. Our radios and television would stop normal broadcasts with "This is a test, only a test."

When our parents traveled with us as teenagers, a civil defense warning should have gone off. Dennis was thirteen, working out daily with barbells. He agreed to travel with the family to Pennsylvania only under the condition that the barbells traveled with him.

The lime green, two-toned 1964 Chevrolet Bel Air nearly popped a "wheelie" as an extra 140 pounds of lead was added to the trunk. Grumbling under his breath, Dad begrudgingly squeezed all of our luggage around Dennis's Gold Gym just so he didn't disrupt his sacred, daily workout.

As we ALL went through our own teenage stages, Mom and Dad reflected back on those family vacations. *"You couldn't stand to be in a closed-up hotel, train, much less the Chevrolet with the rest of us idiots. You didn't roll well with the punches. Problems and little obstacles were grossly exaggerated. Survival meant getting back home. And the only time everybody was happy was when you were fast asleep."*

If Mom and Dad had to do it all over again, these are the things they would do:

- They would plan activities that included everyone, especially in all the sensory experiences.
- They would not organize family vacations so rigidly, leaving out spontaneous, memory-making moments.
- Since teenagers are at the know-it-all stage, they would put them in charge of directions.
- They would include the teens in planning and budgeting the family vacation.

AND AT THE END OF THE JOURNEY . . .

Be flexible with testy teenagers and give them responsibilities as fellow family travelers.

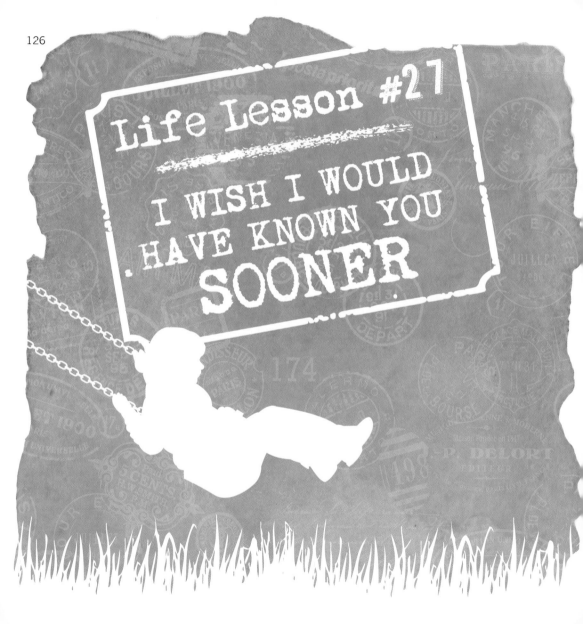

Grandparents Sam and Deb were babysitting their grandchildren for the weekend, giving their son and daughter-in-law a well-deserved break.

The subject of family vacations came up, and Deb started sharing her fondest memories of traveling with her own sister and parents. "In the wintertime, we would go to our grandparents' farm, about 120 miles to the north of Concord, New Hampshire. There my sister and I would always find new things to do in the snow, but our favorite winter vacation activity was skating on Granddad's pond."

In the summertime, Deb and her sister would spend their summer vacation returning to that same farm. Granddad had two swings. One hung from the elm tree in the front yard and the other was a rope swing positioned just south of the lake. They spent hours swinging on both, but their favorite memories were both swinging together high over the pond and dropping simultaneously to make a giant splash.

"Oh, and did I tell you that Granddad got a pony for us to ride any time we wanted to hop on. We even rode Butternut to catch fireflies in Grandma's jelly jars." Mesmerized by Deb's story, her four-year-old grandson Samuel chimed in, "I sure wish I would have gotten to know you sooner."

So it goes that the sweetest memories of family vacations are often about the simplest things in life.

"Grandpa is the smartest man on this planet! He teaches me good things but I don't get to see him enough to get as smart as him."—Kevin (age seven)

AND AT THE END OF THE JOURNEY . . .

Share your childhood vacation stories with your grandchildren.

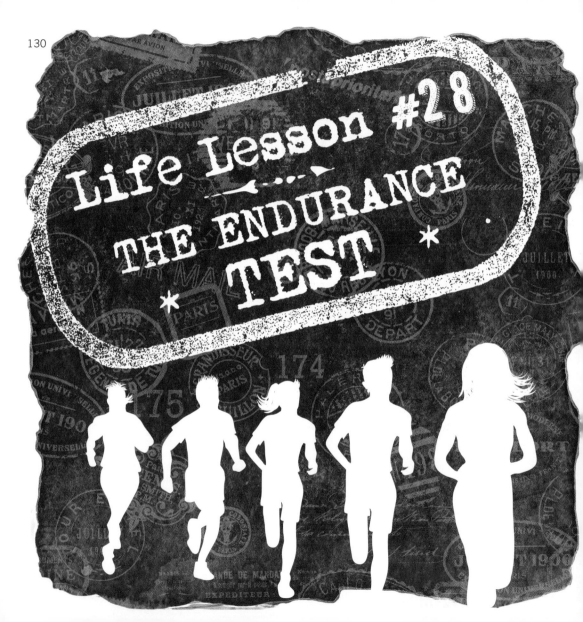

Life Lesson #28

THE ENDURANCE TEST

Our vacations were more like endurance tests than times of rest and relaxation.

Back in the 1960s, Tocquigny vacations always began in the wee dark hours of Sherman, Texas, long before the roosters crowed at the Spanglers' house on Harrison Street. Dad didn't even get up that early for work.

My dad thought an early exodus from 307 North Grand would give us a perfect start, so our vacation started when the sun rays met the Texas horizon. Putting in 180 miles early gave Dad a sense of "vacation accomplishment."

The ritual was always the same: pack the car the night before, have the car serviced and fueled up, wash the windshield for meticulous clarity, wake the family of six in stages, eat Mom's scrambled eggs, grab your pillows, grab your games to play, take your battle stations in the car, and off we drove down US Highway 75.

As Walker Moore says, "I'm glad my parents never took us to Israel. It would have been called the 'We Ran Where Jesus Walked Tour.' No doubt we would have beaten the two Marys to the empty tomb."

My parents determined the success of each vacation day by how many miles we drove and how many sights we viewed within each twenty-four-hour period. To this day, I don't know how we saw Oakmont Nuclear Plant, the Grand Ole Opry, and Smoky Mountain National Park all in the same day, but Mom and Dad considered that a vacation triumph. Chalk it up for the great teachers at Jefferson Elementary, the Tocquigny clan was a bunch of counters. We were so good at counting, our picture appeared in the local newspaper, the *Sherman Democrat*, for counting cars on Grand Avenue.

We have realized that the traditions of our family vacation were passed down to our daughters. There is no other explanation for waking up the family in the wee hours of the morning, standing sleepily at the gate of Magic Kingdom, and racing in to ride Space Mountain. Or being the first arrivals to the Schlitterbahn Water Park in New Braunfels, Texas, on opening day and being the last ones down their slides while everyone else has packed and gone home.

"Take it ALL in on vacation!" —Jennifer Tocquigny

AND AT THE END OF THE JOURNEY . . .

Juice your vacation for all the activities you can squeeze in.

Life Lesson #29

STOPPING FOR DIRECTIONS

Once upon a time there was a group of Canadian geese, getting ready for their annual vacation from Calgary to Colorado. Alpha, the husband, asked his wife, Glory, to get the siblings ready. Gerald, Gloria, and the youngest daughter, Gandy, were excited for their upcoming flight with the whole family in the V.

"So I hear that the family next door may be joining us," said Glory. "Honey, did you invite them without letting me know?"

Alpha looked away. "Well, yes, sort of . . . We were talking out in the yard about the grasslands of Colorado and how the winters are getting milder. It's also a shorter distance than going to Lake Tahoe. Besides, that place is getting too many visitors from Toronto and Montreal. You really don't want to be crowded by more Canadians."

There's a time for flight and a time for fight
A time to feed and a time to read
A time to embrace our children and a time to let go
A time to seek and a time to be found
A time to be in crowds and a time to escape from all the V formations

Family vacations always meant great storytelling and visiting places of importance

"Mom, I want to return to my birthplace," said son Gerald.

"Me, too," echoed Gloria.

Gandy asked Mom to tell her the story of how she was born on a lake near Indian Peaks and almost got killed by a human swinging a pitching wedge hitting a round, white, dimpled flying foreign object that nearly clipped her wings.

With the children all fed and well preened, the home nest was secured and the neighbors were notified of their Colorado vacation. Their elderly neighbors would be staying in Calgary since they were no longer able to fly.

And off the runway they left, led by their drafting dad. "Honey, did you happen to get a wind forecast from any of your friends before leaving?"

"Uh, no, but the prevailing winds seem to always favor us during this season."

Glory muttered under her wing, "Sheesh, why do men always think they can get somewhere without detailed information?"Alpha heard and retorted, "We can always stop to ask along the way or even watch traffic flow as we go."

Glory did a great job of keeping the kids occupied for the first leg of the flight. They started getting restless about thirty miles into the trip.

It didn't take long for them to get agitated at each other. Separating the son from the daughters, Alpha suggested that Gerald should come to the front seat.

"Son, check out this view."

"Nice view, Dad! We just passed a great place to stop called Tim Horton's with beautiful green grass . . . and donuts."

"I know—I have seen thirteen of them so far, and we haven't even left the city limits. Remember, Son, when you take your family on a vacation someday, always drive on a full tank of gas. . . . I mean—keep the tummies full, have plenty of places of interest to stop, and keep a log of travel expenses."

As they adventured to the south, the lanes of traffic were subsiding. Finally taking their first break, Alpha landed the family ninety miles slightly southwest of Calgary.

"Stretch those legs, children. Let's get something to munch on and refuel."

No longer muttering, Glory honked out, "Is it my imagination, or are we headed to the west?"

Alpha stomped off and asked another guy. "I got the new directions, kids. Dad knows where we are going." After a grazing snack, they took off in an adjusted position and were now on course.

Glory sneered at Alpha and said, "Feeling good about yourself now?"

"Yeah, I'm glad we are going the right direction. I sensed we should not have veered off on I-40 west. Sure, honey, you are always right."

"Getting lost may turn out to be the most memorable part of a family vacation."
—Rick Tocquigny

AND AT THE END
OF THE JOURNEY . . .

Plan on getting lost
and enjoying it.

SECTION FIVE
HOW YOU TRAVEL MATTERS

Life Lesson #30

A GIVING COMMUNITY

In a small stationery store in Florence, Italy, Carla was looking in the spiral notebook category and saw the funniest duck and broke out in snorting laughter. This mallard had a snorkel, yellow diving mask, and two neon green swimmer fins on his webbed feet. The store had never heard this type of outrageous laughter before!

We purchased the notebook and did research to discover the clever photographer named Chiara Castellini.

Chiara is a free-spirited, creative genius that derives her imagination from nature. Surrounding herself with hedgehogs, rabbits, ducks, and insects of all kinds, she creates art that is considered avant garde, off the grid, and hilarious.

We managed to contact Chiara by e-mail and, through her niece's English translation, formed a lasting relationship that has helped Chiara create a brand presence in America. Our publishing company, Gracefully Yours, now produces Chiara's greeting cards.

Two years after producing Chiara's first greeting card, we traveled to the Castellini home in the lakes region of Italy. Beginning our visit with hugs, we entered her home, which was fragrant with fresh flowers and a beautiful table of hors d'oeuvres. With one of her neighbors by her side, we conversed through her nephew.

We learned about Chiara's passion for art, love of family, and high regard for her friends. As we spoke, a stream of neighbors starting flowing in with various Italian dishes for our lunch. In came a friend with a bowl of fresh-cooked zucchini lightly coated with locally produced olive oil. Another friend swung by with Caprese—sliced tomatoes, basil, and mozzarella cheese. Knocking on the door was a third cousin with a bowl of homegrown strawberries.

Chiara directed us to her kitchen and opened the oven door to reveal pesto lasagna with homemade noodles. Topping it off, another neighbor strolled in with prosciutto-wrapped cantaloupe. Our unexpected feast ended with a delicate Italian pastry and the most extraordinary-tasting cappuccino.

We left Chiara's home to tour her village and visit her studio. We met more friends along the way, engaged in our broken Italian, and got a true sense of this close-knit community. The houses and businesses were physically close, but their relationships were seemingly closer. Chiara's studio was small yet powerfully impressive. We saw her latest creations, a duck wearing a tiara and holding a queen's staff. Where does she get these ideas? Maybe it is spring fed by all the good friends and wonderful food. We ended our visit to the incomparable Chiara with hugs and kisses.

"Pull up a chair. Take a taste. Come join us. Life is so endlessly delicious." —Ruth Reichl

AND AT THE END OF THE JOURNEY . . .

Learn from other communities about the true sense of friendship and hospitality.

Life Lesson #31

* CURIOUS *
SEPARATE
REALITIES

? ? ?

Family vacations created a natural, organic lifestyle of curiosity for our two daughters. To this day, signs are hung in their LA apartments that read, "Stay Curious." Simply put, family vacations have taught them to be interested in the way people live in their separate realities. The concept of separate realities means that the individual differences in our ways of seeing the world prohibit us, the travelers, from seeing their real world. The oppressed farmers of Zimbabwe are abjectly poor and under scrutiny by their government. They are allocated a certain amount of gas to purchase, limited in what they can grow, and under pressure from opposing urbanites. To them, freedom is just another word for nothing left to lose.

We can slip into foreigners' separate realities by becoming more like them, respecting their tradition, and dropping our own self-centeredness. During Ramadan, we can fast with the family, observe their time of ritual, and attempt to blend in. We may never understand their faith, but we can honor their special festivals and value shared humanity. To be a curious traveling family seeking knowledge, you need to be fluid and light footed. Sometimes you just need to be quiet, observe, listen, and learn.

"Try to understand men. If you understand each other you will be kind to each other. Knowing a man well never leads to hate and almost always leads to love."—John Steinbeck

AND AT THE END OF THE JOURNEY . . .

Honor the separate realities of those you visit, deeply respecting your differences.

? ? ?

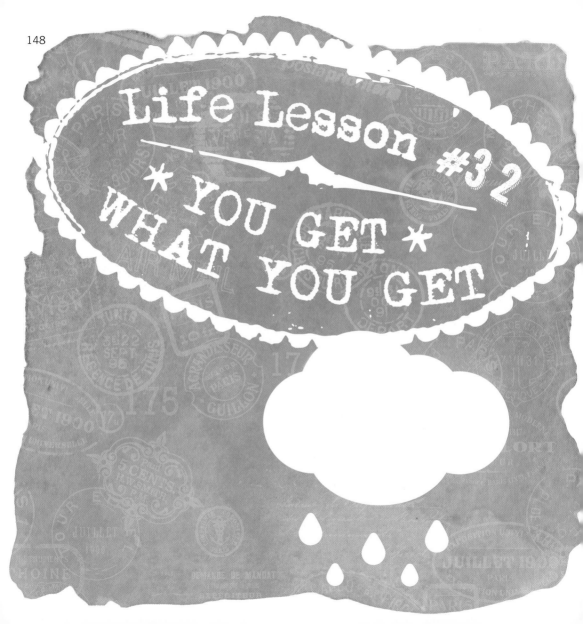

Life Lesson #32

* YOU GET *
WHAT YOU GET

Weather is an important element of an enjoyable family vacation. It can bring forth idyllic conditions with perfect temperatures and a modest breeze. It can also wreak havoc, depending on where you are going and the adventure you are pursuing.

According to *Today Show* weatherman Al Roker, you have to roll with the punches when it comes to weather. He carefully forecasts the weather for America, but as his daughter's elementary school teacher used to say, "you get what you get." While on family vacation, you can't control all the conditions, but you can adopt the right attitude about being together.

A fellow New Yorker, David Morris, remembers the summer of 1976, America's Bicentennial, leaving Los Angeles in their family motor home and heading east on Route 66 for what their dad would describe as "an amazing adventure." With his parents and two sisters, they met the desert heat at the Grand Canyon, searing temperatures at the Alamo, rain and humidity in New Orleans, and clear blue skies at Kennedy Space Center, Florida. The ten-year-old boy took it all in.

The Morris crew continued their adventure up the East Coast, stopping to visit relatives in Georgia, driving the motor home through Manhattan, and eventually landing at Cape Cod. On their tails was Hurricane Belle.

David's dad made a decision to batten down the hatches, not overreact, and sit out the storm. Remembering that scary night, David's emotions ran the gamut from sheer fright to "this is actually pretty cool." As they learned, storms have a mind of their own. Hurricane Belle was no exception. Belle hit New York City and glanced off into the Atlantic, missing Cape Cod and the Morris family.

According to Al Roker, "The best part of the family vacation is that you are together, and the worst part is that you are ALL together, in all weather conditions. The whole vacation experience, combined with unpredictability of weather, teaches tolerance, compromise, and flexibility."

Roker recalls taking family vacations with his five siblings and Mom and Dad in their 1967 Country Squire station wagon. While the Rokers did not take many vacations, the trips they experienced were priceless, especially with Al Sr.

"Dad was a Brooklyn bus driver. He developed the hard left turn maneuver—and we would come sliding across the faux leather seat slamming into each other. This move would keep our behavior in check, especially on family vacations." Fortunately for Al Jr., Dad never pulled this maneuver during a rainstorm.

"Keep family vacations real. You don't need to impress your children. Enjoy togetherness, regardless of the weather." —Al Roker

AND AT THE END OF THE JOURNEY . . .

Count on weather as being one of the memorable elements of your adventure. Good or bad, you get what you get, so don't complain.

Life Lesson #33

THE LITTLE BROWN ICE CHEST

The Little Brown ice chest, a staple on every family vacation in the 1960s, taught our family many lessons.

With a brownish, copper-tone exterior, tin interior for optimal refrigeration, rubber seal, one drain, a bottle opener, ice pick, and aluminum tray, this 21" × 12"× 14" extension of 307 North Grand was a friend to the family.

With its designated place in the garage, it was only used once a year for family vacations. When we saw Dad washing it out, we knew that the time was drawing near to hit the road.

And Little Brownie stunk! With its galvanized interior, the aroma was memorably musty. My job was to scrub out the interior and be ready for our annual trip to the Sherman Ice House.

One of the last check items for the family vacation was to pick up a ten-pound block of ice at the Lamar Avenue icehouse. After the block was purchased, Dad had the responsibility of packing Little Brownie with Cragmont drinks. Mom bought twelve for $1.00 and included the usual cream soda, ginger ale (for upset stomachs), orange, and everybody's favorite, root beer.

Little Brownie was equipped with an ice pick, bottle opener, and a convenient tray to hold Mom's special items for the trip. Dad also packed in milk and condiments for sandwiches, including nasty Miracle Whip and French's mustard. In "Mom's tray" were tomatoes, cheese slices, and a wet washcloth to wipe Dad's sweaty brow. Dad would lock up Little Brownie and tenderly cover it with a towel to keep it cold.

With Little Brownie loaded against the backseat of the '56 two-toned Chevrolet station wagon, the family of six loaded in. Front-seat positions went to Dad—always driving, with no relief, Suzanne (the eldest), and Dennis, the second of three sons. The fourth occupant in the front was Dad's metallic green ashtray that sat strategically on the transmission hump. The backseat went to Georgie (eldest son), Ricky (youngest son), and Mom, who took the battle station to fix the family sandwiches as we drove.

Dennis generally managed the radio, scrolling across the AM dial to find music that pleased everyone. Suzanne and Dad controlled the triangular windows at the front, giving us some needed airflow in the sweltering backseat.

156

What if Little Brownie could speak?

- Please tell me that you actually remember the way to Grandmother's house in Fredericktown, Pennsylvania? I'm getting too old to get lost again.
- Do we always have to carry the stinky cheese from Safeway, sausage with peppercorn, and disgusting olive loaf, on every vacation?
- And you call that parallel parking? It's not that I'm embarrassed, I'm more embarrassed for you.
- Remember the concept of washing me out? Let's explore that a little more.
- Hey, can you take it easy? The kids and I are terrified of your lead foot!
- I'm melting, I'm melting. Can you get air-conditioning in your next Chevrolet? You had better listen to your dad and keep me drained. That will make the ice last longer.
- I think your family's lives are more important than trying to swat that fly on the windshield with the *Sherman Democrat* newspaper!
- *Cough, cough* . . . Dad, do you think you could smoke Camels with filters? You are changing the outer color of ole Little Brownie.
- I'm like your dad. I can be easily drained on these family vacations.

"You can build memories around the simple things that accompany you on family vacation." —Carla Tocquigny

AND AT THE END
OF THE JOURNEY . . .

Great travel companions
are not always in the
form of people.

Life Lesson #34

OBJECTS OF AFFECTION

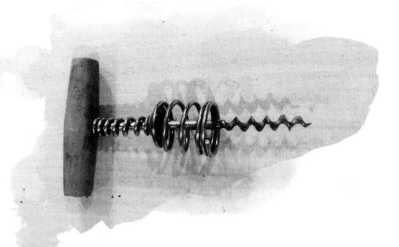

A spring-loaded French corkscrew from the 1890s is a reminder of vacation time with my dad. It wasn't a tool to open a bottle of wine. This one was a keepsake.

Outside of Quebec City, my dad and I made a game of racing into antique stores to find corkscrews, the antique collection we famously had in common. The score was 742 to 612. Dad was leading as we jumped from the driver's seat and front-passenger position into this tiny French Canadian retailer.

We swept the store, eyes darting up and down, east and west, seeking to add to our collection. Muttering as we exited, "It looks like some crazy collectors have beat us to the punch."

Dad did an about-face and asked the shop proprietor, *"Tire-bouchon?"* *"Oui . . . suivez-moi"* ["Yes . . . follow me"]. This petite man of French heritage opened a drawer near his dusty back office and pulled out a rare, spring-loaded corkscrew that we both battled over. Dad won. He spoke better French.

To this day, that singular corkscrew, among the fourteen hundred that were once possessed, remains a prized memory of the father-son interaction on family vacations. While it may seem meaningless to others, it has a story to tell about time together, shared passions, and a unique competitive spirit.

Vacation heirlooms are worth creating and keeping. Once your parents are gone, these little objects of affection hold family vacation memories close to your heart.

"Different people value different things. What is one man's garbage is another man's riches." —Anonymous

AND AT THE END OF THE JOURNEY . . .

Value the treasures of the heart collected on the way of a family vacation.

Life Lesson #35

CHANGE YOUR PLACE AND CHANGE YOUR * HAPPINESS *

樂

HAPPINESS

Like ancient mariners, we have sailed to many continents, often imagining that the brightest-shining stars guide us to the happiest people on earth.

Happy friends in Reykjavik, Iceland, would say if you are happy and you know it, eat some of our fish! They do it almost every day. We wonder if their happiness on this moonlike island comes from fish oil. Ron, a restaurant owner, self-taught chef, and soccer referee for the Europa League, showed us his form of contentment. He always has friends surrounding him, plenty of food to eat, and he provides his guests samples of different Icelandic seafood that his cooks have prepared for lunch. If food is the secret to finding happiness, Ron has tapped into the vein. Travel on down the road to the Blue Lagoon, and the mood is far from blue. In this feel-good spa for thousands, you pay a ticket and find instant relief in the one-hundred-degree pool.

The extra punch of happiness comes from slathering therapeutic mud all over your face and body. The love language of touch was definitely fulfilled from the bottom of this liquid sauna.

Salzburg was anything but an old salt mine. As the center of Mozart's life and the film site for *The Sound of Music*, this gorgeous Austrian city exudes happiness. The townspeople walk about with a genuine sense of glee. The beds seem a little more comfortable, a bowl of goulash is even tastier, and the music that flows from all corners of the city whispers happy.

Salvador, Brazil, celebrates St. Barbara and all the days that shoulder this event. The residents are over-the-top happy, sharing their native foods, and they treated us as extended family. The essential ingredients for their good life start with family, move to faith, and then spread to the community at large. With happiness pumping through their hearts, they teach you their traditional dance and revel in their culture. There are seemingly no strangers in this town.

"One's destination is never a place, but a new way of seeing things." —Henry Miller

AND AT THE END OF THE JOURNEY . . .

Seek out the
happiest people.

樂

HAPPINESS

Life Lesson #36

WORKING VACATIONS

Combining family vacations with work is often a perilous act. In 1966, our family took a vacation to Washington, D.C., where my dad spent part of the trip interviewing for a U.S. government foreign agency position in Nicaragua.

Dad carefully planned the trip so his work would not interfere with our sightseeing. He treated the family to our nicest hotel stay ever on the expense account of Uncle Sam. We all remember the day he climbed the steps to the State Department carrying his briefcase with the GJT insignia (George Joseph Tocquigny). He successfully secured the job, but later confided that his assignment to Nicaragua to help their school system was a "kitchen full of broken dishes."

"Every time we would make a little progress with the Nicaraguan schools, there would be a costly disaster waiting to happen. You would build a new wall and the rest of a school would collapse."

Our Washington, D.C., experience was like Nicky and Tacy Collini's, who combined work and vacationing in a long, long trailer home. Wanting to acquire a large trailer home to travel around the United States to civil engineering projects on which Nicky was employed, they purchased a 1953 thirty-six-foot Redman "New Moon" model (which sold for $5,345 at the time).

Money spent on this working vacation plan continued to mount as Nicky and Tacy had to purchase a more powerful car, equipped with a 125 horsepower, V-8 engine to tow the trailer. Their trip to the Sierra Nevada mountains rapidly became a catalog of disasters, including a rocking trailer around a hairpin turn, which caused the kitchen dishes to crash and break.

After they arrived at the home of Tacy's aunt and uncle, with other relatives and neighbors who were gathered watching, Nicky accidentally backed the trailer into their hosts' carport, partly destroying it as well as a prized rosebush. Later, after turning onto an old logging road at night, Nicky tried to level the trailer while stuck in the mud during a rainstorm. Relations deteriorated within the vacationing family, and finally Tacy stormed off in a huff. In the end, they were tearfully reunited.

Family vacations are full of drama, especially work-related vacations like Nicky's (played by Desi Arnaz) and Tacy's (played by Lucille Ball) in the 1954 feature film *The Long, Long Trailer*. Filmgoers enjoyed a vacation through cinema for just twenty-five cents and watched someone else's mayhem. This movie gave us a future glimpse of our own comedic family vacations to national parks like the Smoky Mountains and Rocky Mountains.

For many, the movie was their first glance at Pines to Palms Scenic Byway—State Road 74—in Palm Desert, California, or the tunnel view where the family emerges to a view of Yosemite Valley, complete with the panorama of El Capitan.

As Nicky and Tacy learned, the best family vacations may end in broken dishes, but they often form the greatest bonds of togetherness through a lifetime of memories.

"Everything right is wrong again."
—From *The Long, Long Trailer*

AND AT THE END OF THE JOURNEY . . .

Create more adventure in your life by combining work with family vacations.

Life Lesson #37

IT'S DOLLARS TO DOUGHNUTS AT OUR STATE FAIR

Growing up in north Texas, we would take short family vacations each autumn to the great State Fair of Texas. There, we learned the fine art of people watching, seeing the newest automobiles, and watching the fanatics from the University of Oklahoma and Texas University collide in crimson and orange.

When the family did not have any money for trips, and that was more often than not, the state fair represented a reprieve from the routine of our hometown. Mom and Dad made sure that we saw the official ribbon cutting that opened the fair. It always corresponded with "Sherman Day" when the Bearcat band would march through the main boulevard of buildings past the Women's Pavilion and the seventy-foot-tall Big Tex statue.

We were curious onlookers mystified by the Automotive Building. We always headed first to see the latest Ford Mustang and Chevy Corvette. Predictably, the show always exhibited a car of the future that included a flying vehicle or one that ran off electricity. We were watching *The Jetsons* on television during that time, which made these inventions more relevant and interesting.

The charm and nostalgia of this state fair, and perhaps your own, brings back memories of a more innocent time of happiness. Grandparents and parents return each year to relive days of yesteryear, delighting their own children with 4-H exhibits and the Food Pavilion.

Understanding the human quest for achievement and the ultimate award of winning a blue ribbon at your state fair, one has to wonder how much positive parent-child interaction time state fairs created with these competitions. Going as a family unit to see how you fared, turning the corner to your exhibit, and seeing your name and a ribbon placed next to your efforts is a milestone moment for many a person. That spirit of competition and achievement is timeless.

As a nation of families, our yearning for yesterdays can often be satisfied with short family vacations. Going to the places we enjoyed in our youth brings back a time when we were all together, away from home if only for a few hours, seeing strange-looking people of all shapes and sizes on the midway. Seeing the birth of fried corn dogs and now witnessing "fried everything."

"If you ever start feeling like you have the goofiest, craziest, most dysfunctional family in the world, all you have to do is go to a state fair. In five minutes at the fair, you'll be going, 'You know, we're all right. We are dang near royalty.'"
—Jeff Foxworthy

AND AT THE END OF THE JOURNEY . . .

Embrace little adventures and relive your youth. Just don't eat the fried Twinkies at your state fair.

Life Lesson #38
TRAVEL FOR GOOD HEALTH

Ever since the discovery of healing waters and hot springs bubbling up from our earth, family vacations have been taken for health reasons. In the 1800s, international travel grew dramatically due to European spas.

Today, Iceland has become a popular place for the entire family to linger in the Blue Lagoon's hundred-degree thermal pools. Family trips to Bath, England; New Zealand; or Turkey help clear up everything from acne to psoriasis.

Visiting Spain, our family learned the art of cooking tapas, eating less, and enjoying food more. Small portions of the right food, especially accentuated by spectacular olive oil, corrected our diet FOR LIFE.

In Germany, we rode bicycles everywhere and got into better physical shape. The air was fresher because of less pollution. Add to that, we slept better at night because we had exercised all day.

You can get the workouts of your life by zip lining in Costa Rica; hiking the Inca Trail in Peru; canoeing at your nearest river; swimming at your local lake, or perhaps one of the GREAT ones; snorkeling in Hawaii or Belize; or white-water rafting down the Arkansas River or maybe the Zambezi.

In Australia, we dined on the very freshest fish we've ever eaten. We consumed it for lunch and dinner; we couldn't get enough of it, lost weight, and felt better about our physique. Exposure to new seasonings from New Mexico, Istanbul, or Bangkok has revved up our metabolism, especially the chilies from our neighboring city to the south, Santa Fe.

In Lake Garda, Italy, we shared meals with families eating vegetables only. Despite our carnivorous ways, these dinners showed us how well you can eat.

In Sweden, we drank more water. It was free and tasted fresher. Staying hydrated made us feel better.

"If I want to go on a diet, I'm off to Granada, Spain." —Carla Tocquigny

AND AT THE END OF THE JOURNEY . . .

Improve your health with travel.

Life Lesson #39

THE WORLD NEEDS YOUR
RANDOM ACTS
OF KINDNESS

"Everyone thinks of changing humanity and nobody thinks of changing themselves." —Leo Tolstoy

Adventure to other countries with your family, and you will see that overall, Americans have very privileged lives.

There was never a better place to practice random acts of kindness than while visiting ravaged areas of Zimbabwe. We had never seen an area so poverty stricken. At the street market in Harare, our family saw maimed children, men without arms or legs, and destitute beggars. You can imagine the gesture of a tiny gift, money to eat for a month, or an object to build self-esteem.

To our surprise, our little random acts set in motion a series of kind acts by other visitors to Harare. People started opening up their pocketbooks and purses, giving out of the goodness of their hearts. As if there were a higher calling, there was a positive feeling at the marketplace that day, reminding us of the most important elements of life—service to others, kindness to our fellow man, and compassion.

By giving away food, we gain strength; by bestowing gifts on others, we gain more inner beauty; by donating material things, we acquire treasures of our own.

On all future family vacations, our daughters would pack gifts to give away. Without any prompts from Mom or Dad, these random acts of giving were coming from their hearts. They included making hair ribbons, buying toys, and creating small stashes of money to give away anonymously.

Perhaps there is a larger purpose to family vacations where we are tested to see, understand, and act. Traveling together can shape the character of our children, and perhaps the parents, too.

"The fragrance always remains in the hand that gives the rose." —Gandhi

AND AT THE END OF THE JOURNEY . . .

Introduce random acts of kindness on your family vacation.

Life Lesson #40

* HISTORY *
COMES TO LIFE

Hiking Trails

Vacations can be as simple as hiking the trails in your nearest national park. However, learning that the trail you experienced was carved out by settlers in the 1800s on the settlers' journey to the West can bring that trail into a whole new light.

We were prepping for an overseas trip when our daughters were reading books on the Holocaust for world literature class. A trip was planned to Dachau to see history, even history at its worst. Their insightful knowledge made the trip more meaningful and tearful.

A few years later, both daughters were taking art history classes in college. We visited the Louvre, Uffizi, and MOMA to see in person the art they had studied. Having written essay papers on Michelangelo's life before visiting Florence gave them a greater appreciation of this incredible artist's life and passion. They even visited where he was born and grew up as a teenager.

Whether you go on a quest to travel like Lewis and Clark along the Columbia River or follow the trail to see Michelangelo's carvings in Europe, your journey as a family will be enhanced if you read, learn, and absorb information about the people who traveled before you.

"Certainly, travel is more than the seeing of sights and relearning history; it is a change that goes on, deep and permanent, in the ideas of living." —Miriam Beard

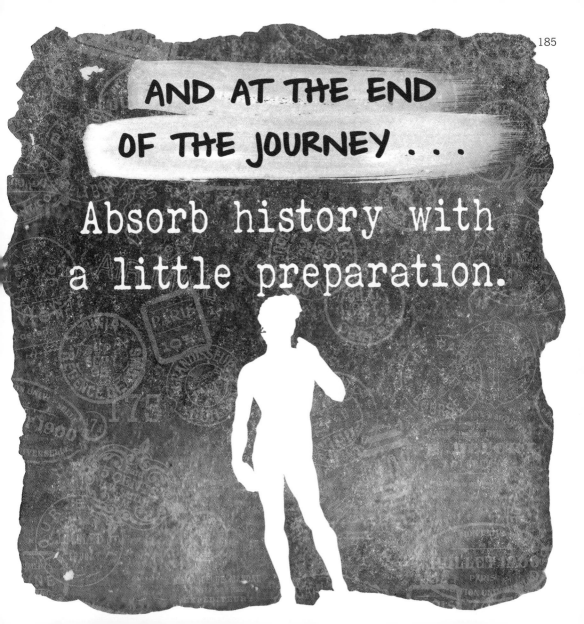

AND AT THE END OF THE JOURNEY . . .

Absorb history with a little preparation.

Life Lesson #41

THE PURSUIT OF * TASTEFUL * KNOWLEDGE

"The pursuit of knowledge is like exploring a new continent, an adventure for the soul." —Anatole France

Family vacations have taught us the art of enjoying culture. The aim of traveling with your loved ones, among many idealistic goals, is the development of good taste in knowledge and good form in conduct.

The well-traveled family is not necessarily a unit of people who are well read, privileged, or learned, but a group who likes and dislikes the right things. As Lin Yutang would say, "To know what to love and what to hate is to have taste in knowledge."

Throughout the course of travels, especially to Italy, we know people who know every topic and can ramble through the course of conversation with factoids on every topic.

These same people generally hold a weak point of view on nearly every subject. Consider the great historians who tour families through the Sistine Chapel. Through fastidious scholarship, they drone on with statistics about the marble used to sculpt the *Pietà* but lack the story about why Michelangelo was inspired with this creation. Such a person lacks a taste in knowledge.

The easiest task is to accumulate knowledge, but a discerning traveler is an archaeologist for the deeper meaning of people and their environment.

"My life is limited, while knowledge is limitless."
—Chuang Tzu

AND AT THE END OF THE JOURNEY . . .

Put emphasis on the spirit of exploration and learning. The pursuit of knowledge is not just in the facts, but in the experience.

Life Lesson #42

BODY CLOCKS

JET LAG (noun, 1969): extreme fatigue and crankiness felt by a family after a long flight across several time zones; results from disruption of circadian rhythms of Mom, Dad, and children.

Doctors say that when you cross a singular time zone, your body will feel a lag of one full day. Crossing multiple time zones can jar your family vacation, knocking out the "power lines" for a few days.

Despite a significant amount of family vacations, we are still learning.

- If you are jet lagged, you've probably consumed your weight in Dunkin' Donuts; CBTL, Caribou, or Starbucks coffee, and to no effect.
- Your smart phone, watch, iPad, or laptop all show different times, and you don't know which to believe. Don't count on your body clock. It's of zero help.
- Your children and teenagers can now fall asleep anywhere, at any time.
- While on tours of notable jungles, you are yawning so much that local insects think you are a new, welcomed cave.
- Your family feels disoriented at all meals with half wanting breakfast and the other half feeling like it's dinnertime.
- You keep greeting people with the wrong "day part" phrase. You say good morning and it's 7:30 at night.
- Expect the unexpected emotional outburst from any member of the family. Sleep deprivation will cause scenes from *The Exorcist*.
- Airports are the only place your family fits in. Other people look equally tossed and tumbled.
- Pulling an all-nighter and letting everyone binge watch TV and movies is ill advised.

- At some point, your kids' brains kick into third gear while yours are fading. They ask questions that you can't answer: Why do we have time zones anyway?
- Everyone you meet, including travel experts from Frommer's, Lonely Planet, *New York Times*, and Rick Steves have their own expert opinion on how to alleviate their own jet lag. They never address FAMILIES on vacation.

Here are some of our tips:
(a) Take the right dosage of melatonin.
(b) Bring along a pillow for in flight.
(c) Hydrate.
(d) Get to bed earlier during the week preceding the trip.
(e) Recharge with a nap at your new destination.

"Twenty years from now you will be more disappointed by the things that you didn't do than by the ones you did do. So throw off the bowlines. Sail away from the safe harbor. Catch the trade winds in your sails. Explore. Dream. Discover." —Mark Twain

AND AT THE END OF THE JOURNEY . . .

Prepare and adapt your family for jet lag.

Life Lesson #43

TREATING OTHERS LIKE FAMILY

In our endeavors to find local lodging wherever we travel, we did an Internet search for a planned trip to Santiago, Chile. Instead of a high-rise hotel, we discovered a bed-and-breakfast on a shaded backstreet of downtown Santiago named De Blasis.

We delighted in meeting Andres, the young owner and B and B proprietor, who prided himself in the open windows and hospitality of De Blasis. The twenty-nine-year-old played the veritable Chilean host, giving us explicit directions to his favorite grocery store and local restaurants.

Born with a friendly disposition and heart for travelers, Andres willingly answered all of our questions and sent us on a side jaunt to Santa Cruz to tour the famed Chilean wine country. Knowing that we were avid collectors of corkscrews, he gave us specific directions to an antique mall where we discovered and purchased a rare *tire-bouchon* featuring the likeness of French president Charles de Gaulle. Every time we look at this prized collector's item, we think of Andres.

We found out the secret to Andres. He learned an important lesson from his mom that guests should always be treated like family. She engendered a core value that Andres applies every day—little things really matter. They all add up to a great experience.

"How people treat other people is a direct reflection of how they feel about themselves." —Drake

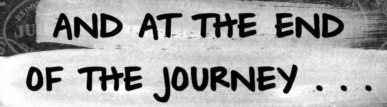

AND AT THE END OF THE JOURNEY . . .

Seek out places where you are treated like family.

SECTION SIX
THE NEXT JOURNEY

Life Lesson #44

IT'S TIME FOR A FAMILY VACATION

By now you know that nothing says happiness like a good ole vacation. If you haven't taken a trip with your loved ones in a while, then it's time! Here are nine sure signs that you are overdue for a family vacation:

- You are annoyed by the Christmas cards and letters that tell you about where your friends and family are vacationing.
- Traffic jams have become such a regular part of your daily routine that they no longer upset you.
- You download stunning pictures of dreamy vacation spots and put them on your Facebook home page.
- Your passport has to be dusted off with a Swiffer.
- Your selfies are from your local town while others have the Golden Gate Bridge or Egyptian pyramids (look again, maybe that was the Luxor in Las Vegas).
- Your favorite Samsonite or Baggallini still has the flight tag from five years ago.
- You buy souvenirs online and can't remember the last souvenir purchased at a real location.

- You ask the offspring where they would like to go. You can't get a consensus on the destination, but everyone is ready to leave—for anywhere—tomorrow.
- You daydream while posting travel photos on your Pinterest board.

"Why should a family save money? To go on vacation!!" —Peter (age five)

AND AT THE END OF THE JOURNEY . . .

Make the time to take family vacations.

Awaken your five senses and be transformed
Be curious
Create lifetime memories
Discover the rest of the world
Engage with the locals
Feel the texture of an ancient sculpture
Go outside your comfort zone
Hike a rugged, unexplored path
Ignite your taste buds
Journey off the road
Keep a journal
Listen to different sounds
Meander
Nourish your thirst for knowledge
Open your nose to new aromas
People watch
Quench your thirst for risk taking
Relish your adventure
Savor unusual people
Travel often; you have the rest of your life to work
Unplug from the rest of the world
View other vistas
Wander
eXplore the globe
Yearn to learn
Zip through work, slow down when you travel

Life Lesson #46

IMPERMANENCE

Our family was emotionally struck by a sign we saw in Mexico, Easter Sunday 2005. We had just received a call from my sister, Suzanne, that Dad had passed away. The sign said, "Don't waste your life."

At milestone moments like this, we realize our impermanence. If we are only given a certain number of days in this life, why not travel with family?

Pema Chodron muses that "life is very brief. Even if we live to be a hundred, it's very brief. And life is very unpredictable. Our lives are impermanent. I myself have, at the most, thirty more years to live, maybe thirty-five, but that would be tops. Maybe I have only twenty more years to live. It's sobering to me to think that I don't have all that long left. It makes me feel that I want to use it well. If you realize that you don't have that many more years to live and if you live your life as if you actually only had a day left, then the sense of impermanence heightens that feeling of preciousness and gratitude."*

"To dedicate a single day to travel with family is a day well spent." —Rick Tocquigny

*Pema Chodron, *The Wisdom of No Escape* (Boston: Shambhala, 1991).

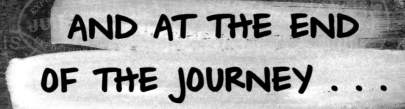

AND AT THE END OF THE JOURNEY . . .

Use your time well by traveling with your loved ones.

Life Lesson #47

CHOOSE WISELY—THIS COULD BE YOUR LAST FAMILY VACATION

It had been three years since the passing of Charlie, a very special dad and husband. He had spent the last ten years of his life suffering from Huntington's disease. Janell, his wife and dedicated caregiver, Carla and Nancy's mom and grandmother to Heather and Jennifer, had not enjoyed a vacation for over a decade.

Carla did her usual due diligence about potential places to go, adventures to pursue, and then began checking the family's busy lives and calendars to coordinate a family vacation. Settling on Cabo San Lucas, Mexico, Carla engineered this outing with two adult daughters in LA, a sister in Austin, her mother, and the two of us from Colorado. Little did she know that this was the last family vacation with our extended family.

Lessons learned from planning this trip were many and stand the test of time.

- Travel NOW. You never know if this is the last vacation. You and your loved ones are not going to live forever.
- Keep your plans simple and manageable. You can go to a destination that is exotic in your own country or hemisphere. Keep your air time or drive time to under three hours.

- Be respectful of walking distance. If wheelchairs are not available, your selection of hotels should always include spacious elevators.
- Research the towns you will be visiting for wheelchair "friendliness." Use TripAdvisor to check out the ease of navigating prospective locations. Hint—don't plan on visiting Eze, France, unless you want to shake up your relatives on their cobblestone streets.

On a pathway to the port of Cabo, we experienced a runaway wheelchair with Janell. The ramp was unexpected, and we nearly baptized her in the Gulf of Mexico. She wasn't expecting an amusement park ride on this vacation. Yes, Janell survived and laughs to this day about the incident.

- Hotel selections mean picking the right kind of bathtub with handicap-accessible bars. Be mindful of special "happy must-haves." We have actually had to pry Dad out of a bathtub that was not equipped with pull-up bars. We laugh about the incident now, but at the time, it wasn't pretty!

- Minimize travel hassles and extra movement with nonstop flights. Keep the travel process simple for your family by picking a destination that is easy to reach and doesn't leave your family exhausted upon arrival.
- Pace yourself to the slowest family member. Remember that you are not on family vacation to receive a trophy for the most rides ridden at Disney World in a single day. You should plan your sightseeing days with ample time to meander and linger at the pace of the eldest member. This will require managing the expectations of the youngest travelers on this trip. Tell them ahead of time what to expect.
- Take the Boy Scout oath on steroids. Be doubly prepared for all health emergencies with medication, hydrocortisone, Advil, sty medicine, and plenty of Purell.
- Plan your location for meals. Understand that everyone gets hungry (and cranky) on their own clock. When eating out, anticipate the entire family's needs, budget, and desire for different dining experiences. You can manage grumbling stomachs with healthy snacks and bottled water to fill the gaps in between meals. You may be traveling with family that grazes eight times a day. Don't criticize their eating habits, but lean into their cycle by offering something to keep their mouth moving.

- Take photos of the little moments. You will cherish photos of Grandmother and her granddaughters sharing a dessert or a quiet moment together on the beach.

"So if a person lives many years, let him rejoice in them all." —Ecclesiastes 11:8

AND AT THE END OF THE JOURNEY . . .

Make every vacation count.

Life Lesson #48

GREAT TRIP, DAD, WHERE TO NEXT?

Family vacations have made our kids addicted to travel. We don't think there is a cure for their wanderlust.

Every family trip creates another insatiable hunger to see someplace new, meet new people, hear new sounds, taste different foods, and grow in knowledge. Luring you further and further, each new journey infects the family for more travel together.

Lately, the art of taking a trip has grown "extended legs." If we are headed to Southeast Asia for a specific trip to Vietnam and Cambodia, the attitude is "Why not fly two hours south to Bangkok and take a cooking class?"

Invariably, as each trip ends, one of the daughters is already asking about next time. When asked for their suggestion, one says Sydney and the other says Patagonia. Why there? If anyone in the family answers, "Because it's there," you have moved from traveling with family to traveling with a bunch of adventure junkies.

We attribute the family wanderlust to a special genetic strain from Petie Tocquigny, Army Air Corps nurse in World War II, consummate globe-trotter, mother, and grandmother. Our trips have all been about full engagement, sensory awakening, and life transformation.

Wanderlust is habit forming when you find great people to lodge with in their homes—like James the luthier in Cremona, Italy. And wanderlust is fed by cooking with characters—like Elena Nappa at Borgo Argenina in Castellina in Chianti, Italy.

The biggest wanderlust high comes when you are blessed with a ride from Ljubljana, Slovenia, to Trieste, Italy, out of the kindness of someone's heart.

As you write the final details in your travel journal, finish a scrapbook, or post that final picture on social media, you have a special glow about your persona. Now you know why travel is such a life-altering activity.

"Every time I look up and see a plane in the sky, I dream of somewhere new." —Phil Keoghan, Host, *The Amazing Race*

AND AT THE END OF THE JOURNEY . . .

Start planning your next trip right after your family returns from vacation.
Feed the addiction!

Life Lesson #49

WRITING THEIR OWN TRAVEL STORIES

From the beginning of our family vacations, our children learned how to travel through their five senses. They were fearless conversationalists talking with the owners of a Seefeld, Austria, bed-and-breakfast as we shared a delicious meal. They loved sitting by a stream, whittling on a stick, smelling the columbines, and listening to the robins in the aspen trees of Estes Park, Colorado.

A lifetime of memorable travel is ingrained into the souls of Heather and Jennifer Tocquigny. In 2013, Heather purchased a one-way ticket to Granada, Spain, to learn Spanish. Staying in the home of Rosa, this woman would be her "madre" for the two months that she studied in Spain.

Spanish was not all that Heather learned, however. Honing her cooking skills in this tiny kitchen, from Rosa's expertise, Heather learned how to create *delicioso* tapas with just a couple of ingredients. Riding the bus to new locations around Spain and Portugal with new acquaintances, Heather pursued her passion of photography and created lifetime friends.

Jennifer has flown solo to Nairobi twice and spent a week teaching art at Grace Orphanage outside the city. The children loved the bows that she crafted for them! Living with the owners of the orphanage and walking to the compound on the dusty road each day with lumbering giraffes along her side, travel has transformed her. Having volunteered in 2012 and 2014, Jennifer's perspective has been permanently altered. Travel has taught her happiness and a deeper appreciation for family and for the simple things in life like clean, running water.

Their journey continues, founded on the travel lessons they learned from our family vacations over the years.

We taught our daughters to travel as transformed travelers. The lessons we taught them can manifest themselves in YOUR children, too.

"Traveling can leave you speechless and then turn you into a storyteller." —Rick Tocquigny

AND AT THE END
OF THE JOURNEY . . .

Teach your children well
so they become wonderful
transformed travelers.
Where to next??

EPILOGUE

We hope that you have enjoyed traveling with us in *Life Lessons from Family Vacations*. Each story was written for your reading enjoyment and to help you become a little more mindful of the unique lessons coming from your own travels.

We encourage you to travel with family, especially with extended family of grandparents, uncles, aunts, and cousins, whether it is across town, to the next county, to another state, to a nearby beach, or even to a foreign country.

Not only should you take the time, but you should make the time for family vacations. We think it is the best investment in life.

And at the end of your journey, we hope you discover your own life lessons and perhaps get closer to understanding yourself, your loved ones, and the world around you.

Rick Tocquigny is cofounder of **Artbeat Media** and www.gracefully-yours.com greeting card publishing. A graduate of Texas A&M University, he hosts the popular podcasts *Transformed Traveler*, *Life Lessons*, and *Mentoring Monday*. Visit www.transformedtraveler.com and www.life-lessons.co and share your life lessons with Rick's team. He resides in Lafayette, Colorado, with his wife, Carla.

Carla Tocquigny is the mother of two globetrotting daughters and cofounder of The Transformed Traveler Network. Having traveled to over 50 countries, her aim in life is to teach adventurous people how to travel through their five senses. Visit www.transformedtraveler.com